ENGLISH in the Lives of DAY LABORERS

TEACHER'S GUIDE

Level 1

CASA of Maryland

English in the Lives of Day Laborers: Teacher's Guide

CASA of Maryland, Inc.
Education and Leadership Department
June 2004

Gustavo Torres
Executive Director

Alexandra Escudero
Chief Operating Officer

Elmer Romero
Education Department Director

Paul Zilly
Research, Methodology, Text, Layout, and Design

German Zepeda
Art Work

Day Laborers of CASA of Maryland
Research, Text, and Photo Credits

The quotes in the margin of this book come from the writings of Paulo Freire (see bibliography).

ISBN 0-9745971-0-4
Library of Congress Control Number: 2003098066

Administrative Office
310 Tulip Ave.
Takoma Park, MD 20912
Tel: (301) 270-3609
Fax: (301) 270-8659

Center for Employment and Leadership
734 University Blvd. E.
Silver Spring, MD 20903
Tel: (301) 431-4185
Fax: (301) 431-4179

Baltimore Center for Workers' Rights
113 S. Broadway
Baltimore, MD 21231
Tel: (410) 732-7777
Fax: (410) 732-2692

www.casademaryland.org

Contents

Contents

Introduction

The purpose of this book is to help Spanish speakers learn the English that they need in their daily lives. It is especially designed for day laborers who, for whatever reason, find themselves in the United States, and need to communicate so they can find work.

The idea for this book started with the students in the English classes at CASA de Maryland along with their teacher, Paul Zilly. In trying to focus on the daily language needs of the workers and their personal experiences, we hope to inspire all people who want to learn English as a second language.

. . . .

El presente libro tiene como objetivo contribuir al aprendizaje del idioma inglés de una manera más práctica para todas aquellas personas habla hispana que por cualquier razón se encuentran en los Estados Unidos y que tienen la necesidad de comunicarse especialmente para buscar un empleo como trabajadores del día.

La idea surgío entre los estudiantes de la clase de inglés de CASA de Maryland con con su profesor Paul Zilly. Se ha tratado de utilizar la mayor parte del lenguaje cotidiano en la vida de los trabajadores tomando en cuenta algunos de las experiencias vividas por los alumnos. Esto se hizo con la idea de motivar a las personas que quieren aprender el inglés.

Julio Grijalva
Hever Cruz Reyes
Alberto Jimenez
Hector "Teto" Mendez
Hector Hernández
Paul Zilly

Using this Book

This book is designed for Latino day laborers and their families so that they can educate and organize themselves to improve their quality of life in the United States. It recognizes that day laborers need good jobs so they can feed their families, a dignified place to look for work where they are respected, and a clear path toward full citizenship. It can be used in an open-entry ESOL program, in workshops, in small group classes, with tutors, and for home study, and should generally be viewed as one resource among many intended to strengthen the Latino immigrant community in this country.

Popular Education: A committee of day laborers from CASA of Maryland participated in the development and creation of this book as a part of a collaborative project. The day laborers met on a weekly basis over the course of several months to brainstorm vocabulary, tell stories, and take photographs of themselves at work. Its origins like its content are based on the Freirian values of popular education. These values include promoting balanced group participation as well as critically analyzing problems confronting our community with the goal of changing the conditions that cause these problems to exist.

Unit Goal: Each unit has a goal that describes in broad terms the thematic content that the group will discuss as a part of the unit. Try to keep the goal in mind as you work through the lessons.

Lessons: The lessons are designed as self-contained workshops that students can enter, participate in, and benefit from at any time. Each lesson contains language objectives, target vocabulary, and activities to fill a two-hour class. These lessons are not meant to restrict creativity, rather to be used as a guide to navigate you into the thematic world of the day laborers.

Themes: The curriculum committee chose themes that it felt were most important to the lives of day laborers. Don't ignore the themes! Thinking critically about them will lead you, as Paulo Freire says, "to become more conscious of your presence in the world."

Codes: Codifying reality is central to problem-posing education. The codes should initiate a dialog about the theme. During the dialog, participants might describe the code, identify or analyze the theme, propose ways to solve the problem, or be reminded of a personal experience they want to share. These are conversations that can be held in the students' native language.

Activities: The activities have been organized in the following way: a warm-up, a dialog about the code, speaking and listening activities, reading and writing activities, a closing activity, and an evaluation. The focus on oral skills at the beginning of the lesson allows students with lower literacy skills to participate equally from start of class.

Materials: Most of the materials the students use in class will be created by the group during the lesson itself. Using authentic materials gives students the power of creating the new language as they learn it.

Student's Workbook: The *Student's Workbook* is designed to accompany this guide. It contains worksheets, dialogs, stories, drawings, and photos taken by day laborers of themselves at work. All of the materials in the *Workbook* come from ideas, stories, and reflections shared during the day laborer curriculum meetings.

Games: The games in this book are, for the most part, traditional ESOL games. Others come from popular education workshops or books by Equipo Maíz (see bibliography). If you are unsure about how to play one of the games, consult ESOL resources in the library or invent your own game. Playing games brings joy, laughter, equality, participation, and learning to the class.

Reflection: At the end each unit, take some time to reflect on your students' progress and on your teaching. Use the reflection worksheet at the end of this book or, better yet, keep a reflection journal to record your thoughts, ideas, and what you learned from the students. Remember that popular education grows out of the unity of reflection and action.

Where we are from

Theme: Culture

Content

Introductions

Our Families

Food

Celebrations

Unit Goal

In this unit, we will discuss aspects of our culture and identity. The purpose of our study is to share and internalize our values and traditions. We will also reflect on how our coming to the U.S. has affected our cultural identity and we will search for ways to strengthen and preserve our traditions and customs in the U.S.

1. Interviewing Each Other

Theme: Culture

Language Objectives

- ✎ be able to introduce ourselves
- ✎ be able to say and write basic greetings

Vocabulary

✍ Hi. My name is _____. I am from _____. I live in _____. etc.

Code

Questions for Dialog

1. Describe

What do we see in the picture?
What is the person with the tape recorder saying?
How do you think the other person will respond?

2. Relate and Interpret

What other questions do you think the interviewer will ask?
How will the person being interviewed respond?
Have you ever interviewed someone or been interviewed? What did you talk about?
What can we learn about if we interview each other in this way?

3. Analyze and Act

What values, customs and traditions do you think the people in the picture share?
Where do you think these values come from?
How can we strengthen and internalize these values and traditions?
How can we teach others about our culture and traditions in the U.S.?

Activities	Materials
Warm-Up: Learn names: Ask participants to form a circle. Pass the koosh ball around the circle saying names . Later, add: "My name is _____."	*koosh ball*
Code: Facilitate a discussion about the photograph on p.10 using the questions for dialog as a guide.	*photograph*
Speaking & Listening *Activity #1: Greetings* 1. Use the picture in the code to elicit greetings from the group. 2. Ask: "What is the first thing you say in English when you meet someone?" 3. Practice common greetings with the koosh ball. *Activity #2: Greetings* 1. Form two concentric circles. 2. Participants face each other and practice greetings. 3. Circles rotate and new pairs introduce themselves. *Activity #3: Introductions* 1. Elicit a few basic questions you ask when you introduce yourself in English. 2. Practice asking and answering with koosh ball. 3. Repeat *Activity #2* with questions.	*picture* *koosh ball* *koosh ball*
Break	
Reading & Writing *Activity #1: Cloze Activity* 1. Ask the group to help you write a simple dialog of two people introducing themselves on the board. 2. Group reads through the dialog chorally and in pairs. 3. Now erase key words in the dialog. 4. Volunteers writ e the words in the blanks. *Activity #2: Biography* 1. Brainstorm a few basic biographical questions you ask when meeting someone and write them on the board. 2. Practice reading the questions chorally. 3. Now invite a volunteer to the front of the class. 4. Group asks him/her the questions on the board. 5. Write down what the volunteer says on the board. 6. Read the story out loud while pointing to the words. 7. Group reads the story chorally and in pairs. 8. Repeat with other volunteers.	
Closing: Form concentric circles that rotate in opposite directions. Participants practice introducing themselves.	
Evaluation: Ask the group: "What did you like about the class? What would you like to work on in other classes?	*koosh ball*

Believing in the people is the first indispensable condition for all change.

2. Thinking about our Families

Theme: Culture

Language Objectives

- be able to talk about our families
- know the vocabulary for family members

Vocabulary

- mother, father, brother, sister, son, daughter, etc.

Code

Questions for Dialog

1. Describe

What do we see in this picture?
What is the person in the picture thinking about?
How do you think he feels?

2. Relate and Interpret

What do you think the person in the picture misses most about his family?
What do you miss most about your families?
How important a role does the family play in our culture?
How are families in our culture different than those in other cultures?

3. Analyze and Act

What cultural values with respect to our families are important to retain in the U.S.?
How can we strengthen our ties to our families?
How can we strengthen and internalize our family traditions and values?

Activities	Materials
Warm-Up: Pass the koosh ball and practice saying: "My name is _____. I'm from _____."	*koosh ball*
Code: Facilitate a discussion about the drawing on p.12 using the questions for dialog to guide you.	*drawing*
Speaking & Listening *Activity #1: Vocabulary* 1. Invite the group to brainstorm family vocabulary. 2. Draw pictures of your family on the board. 3. Point to family members and say: "My mother." etc. 4. Invite volunteers to point to the pictures and say the words. 5. Encourage the group to ask questions about your family. *Activity #2: Picture* 1. Ask participants to draw pictures of their families. 2. Participants show their pictures to a partner. 3. Participants introduce their families to the group.	*paper* *markers*
Break	
Reading & Writing *Activity #1: Family Story* 1. Label your picture with vocabulary: mother, father, etc. 2. Ask participants to label their pictures. 3. Write a few sentences about your family. "This is my mother. Her name is _____." etc. 4. Encourage group to ask questions. 5. Group reads the story chorally. *Activity #2: Family Story* 1. Invite a volunteer to talk about his/her family. 2. Transcribe what he/she says on the board. 3. Encourage the group to ask about the volunteer's family. 4. Group reads aloud what you've written. 5. Repeat with other volunteers.	
Closing: Do the worksheet on page 10 of the Student's Book.	*handout*
Evaluation: Write lesson objectives on the board. Make a check mark next to the ones the group thinks it fulfilled.	

3. Eating at Home and in the U.S.

Theme: Culture

Language Objectives

✎ be able to order food in a restaurant

✎ know the vocabulary for common foods

Vocabulary

✍ chicken, rice, milk, eggs, juice, beans, hamburger, etc.

Code

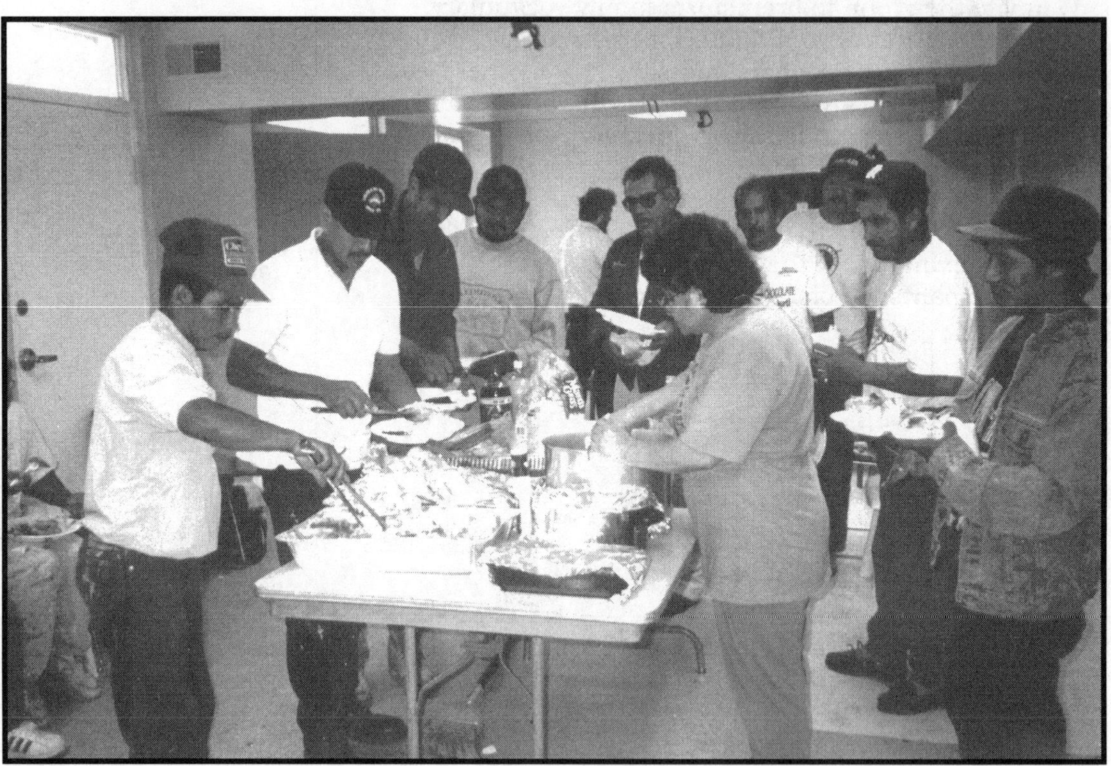

Questions for Dialog

1. Describe

What do we see in this picture?
What are the people in the picture doing?
What kind of food do you think is on the table?

2. Relate and Interpret

What are some traditional foods from our home countries?
How is food back home different from food in other cultures?
Have our eating habits changed since we arrived in the U.S.? In what way?

3. Analyze and Act

What foods do we eat on special holidays in our home countries?
In what other ways is the food we eat related to our culture?
How can we preserve and strenghten our food customs here in the U.S.?

Activities	Materials
Warm-Up: Ball toss: Group members practice saying what food they like: "I like _____."	*koosh ball*
Code: Facilitate a discussion about the photograph on p.14 using the questions for dialog as a guide.	*photograph*
Speaking & Listening *Activity #1: Brainstorm* 1. Ask participants to brainstorm food they eat for lunch and draw pictures of it on the board. 2. Point to the picture and say the names of the food. 3. Invite volunteers to point to the pictures and say the words. 4. Elicit ways of making an order: "I want _____." etc. *Activity #2: Prices* 1. Ask group to set prices for the food drawn on the board. 2. Write the prices on the board next to the pictures. 3. Point to the pictures and ask: "How much is the _____." 4. Invite volunteers to say how much the food items cost. *Activity #3: Role Play* 1. Model a role play between a cashier and a customer. 2. Invite volunteers to play the role of the customer. 3. Group lines up to make a lunch order.	
Break	
Reading & Writing *Activity #1: Menu worksheet* 1. Ask the group to help you write the names of the food next to the pictures on the board. 2. Erase the pictures, point to the words, and read the menu. 3. Group reads the menu chorally. 4. Group does matching exercise on p. 12 of Student's Book. *Activity #2: Dialog Cloze* 1. Invite group to help you write out the food ordering dialog. 2. Group reads the dialog chorally and in pairs. 3. Erase key words in the dialog. 4. Volunteers write in the missing words.	*handout*
Closing: Start a chain drill saying what foods you like and what you don't like: "I like _____, and she likes _____."	*koosh ball*
Evaluation: Ball Toss: "What did you like best about the class?" "What can we improve for classes in the future?"	*koosh ball*

Education is creating a critical spirit, not just transmitting knowledge.

4. Celebrating at Home and in the U.S.

Theme: Culture

Language Objectives

✎ be able to say and write dates in English

✎ be able to say and write the months

Vocabulary

✍ January, February, March, April, etc.

Code

Questions for Dialog

1. Describe

What do we see in this picture?
What is the girl in the picture doing?
What kind of celebration do you think she is dancing at?

2. Relate and Interpret

What culture and traditions are being celebrated in this picture?
Where do you think these traditions come from?
Have you been to a celebration like this one?
What are some traditions from our pueblos?

3. Analyze and Act

What are some other important elements of our culture?
How can we help preserve our traditions and culture in the U.S.?
How can we teach other people about our holidays, history, and culture?

Activities	Materials
Warm-Up: Review the numbers 1-20. Pass out flashcards, form a circle, and practice with koosh ball.	*koosh ball flashcards*
Code: Facilitate a discussion about the photograph on p.16 using the questions for dialog as a guide.	*photograph*
Speaking & Listening *Activity #1: Circle Toss* 1. Show the month on a calendar and ask: "What month is this?" 2. Flip through the calendar, asking: "What month is this?" 3. Write the numbers 1-12 on the board, point to the numbers and ask: "What month is this?" 4. Pass out flashcards 1-12. 5. Form a circle, hold up the flashcards, and toss the ball. 6. Group says the months, chorally and individually. *Activity #2: Dates* 1. Write your name on the board. 2. Next to your name, write your birthdate in numerical form. Point to the numbers and say the date. 3. Ask participants for their birth dates and write them next to their names. 4. Practice saying the dates. 5. Repeat with holidays and other important dates.	*calendar flashcards*
Break	
Reading & Writing *Activity # 1: Matching Game* 1. Write the numbers 1-12 on the board. 2. Invite participants to help you write the months next to the numbers. 3. Group practices reading the months. 4. Now write the abbrieviated form of the months. 5. Group copies the months and abbrieviations onto two sets of index cards. 6. Play matching game with the abbrieviations and the months. *Activity #2: Handout* 1. Guide participants through worksheet on p. 15 of the Student's Book.	*index cards* *handout*
Closing: Dictate some of the dates from the previous activity. Participants practice writing the dates.	
Evaluation: Draw some faces with different expressions on the board. Ask participants how they felt in class.	

Notes

Coming to the U.S.

Theme: Immigration

Content

Coming Here

Feelings

Crossing the Border

Unit Goal

In unit two, we will share stories of coming to the U.S., and we will discuss how immigrating here has affected us, our families, and our communities. We will also analyze the cultural and economic contributions Latinos make when they come to this country and brainstorm ways to ensure that all immigrants are treated with dignity and respect.

1. When Did you Come Here?

Theme: Immigration

Language Objectives

- be able to talk about coming to the U.S. in English
- be able to ask for and give personal information

Vocabulary

- Hi. What's your name? Where are you from? When did you come here? etc.

Code

Questions for Dialog

1. Describe

Who are the people in the picture?
Where are they coming from? Where are they going?

2. Interpret and Relate

Why are the people in the picture coming to the U.S.?
What is the most common reason Latinos cross into the U.S.?
What was the principal reason you came to the U.S.?
What were your experiences crossing the border?

3. Analyze and Act

What economic conditions exist in our countries that force us to leave our homes?
Why do you think these conditions exist?
What contributions do Latino immigrants make to the U.S. economy?
How can we teach others about the contributions we make here?

Activities	Materials
Warm-Up: Ball toss: "My name is _____." When group feels comfortable with this, add: "I live in _____."	*koosh ball*
Code: Facilitate a discussion about the drawing on p. 20 using the questions for dialog as a guide.	*drawing*
Speaking & Listening *Activity #1: Coming to the U.S.* 1. Introduce question words in English: What? Where? etc. 2. Practice saying the question words chorally. 3. Now elicit 1 or 2 simple questions about coming to the U.S. in Spanish: "When did you come here?" for example. 4. Translate the questions into English. 5. Practice asking the questions with the koosh ball. *Activity #2: Group Interview* 1. Elicit answers to the questions. 2. Practice answering the questions chorally. 3. Now divide participants into two groups. One group asks the questions, the other side answers. 4. Switch roles. 5. Invite a volunteer to be interviewed. 6. The group interviews the volunteer. 7. Repeat with other volunteers.	*koosh ball*
Break	
Reading & Writing *Activity #1: Group Interview* 1. Ask the group to help you write the questions on the board. 2. Transcribe the answers to the questions. 3. Practice reading the interview chorally. *Activity #2: Interview in Pairs* 1. Pair up higher level with lower level participants. 2. Pairs interview each other using the questions on the board. 3. Higher level participants transcribe the stories. 4. Pairs share their stories with the class.	
Closing: Divide into smaller groups and play the Coming to the U.S. game on p. 26 of the Student's Book.	*handout*
Evaluation: Draw faces representing how you felt in class today.	

Every thematic investigation which deepens historical awareness is educational.

2. Our Feelings About Coming Here
Theme: Immigration

Language Objectives
- ✎ describe emotional states
- ✎ identify the present tense of "to be"

Vocabulary
- ✍ sad, happy, scared, hungry, angry, etc.

Code

Questions for Dialog

1. Describe
What do we see in the picture?
What are the people in the picture doing?
Where do you think they are from?

2. Interpret and Relate
How do you think they feel to be arriving in a new country?
Why do you think they left their home country?
How do you think they felt when they crossed the border?
How did you feel about leaving your country?

3. Analyze and Act
How has coming to the U.S. affected us and our families?
How has our coming here changed the U.S.? Economically? Culturally?
How can we demonstrate our support of immigrants in this country?

Activities	Materials
Warm-Up: Practice asking and answering, "How are you?" with the koosh ball. Group brainstorms variations of this greeting. Practice variations.	*koosh ball*
Code: Facilitate a discussion about the drawing on p. 22 using the questions for dialog as a guide.	*drawing*
Speaking & Listening *Activity #1: New Vocabulary* 1. Point to the code drawing and ask: "How do they feel?" 2. Tape the picture to the board, point to the picture, and say the emotion. 3. Now ask participants how they think the couple in the drawing felt when they got their first jobs in the U.S. 4. Draw a face representing that emotion on the board. 5. Practice saying the emotion: "Happy", for example. 6. Draw faces with other expressions on the board. 7. Practice saying the emotions. *Activity #2: Group Picture* 1. Ask participants in Spanish how they felt during various stages of their coming to the U.S. (Saying goodbye to their families, crossing the border, getting their first job, etc.) 2. Practice saying these emotions in English. 3. Practice saying: "I was _____." and "She was _____."	*butcher paper* *markers*
Break	
Reading & Writing *Activity #1: Matching Game* 1. Ask group to help you write the emotions next to the faces on the board. 2. Practice reading the new words. 3. Erase the pictures, leaving only the vocabulary words. 4. Say the words; volunteers point to the right word. *Activity #2: Worksheet* 1. Guide participants though exercises on p.24 of the Student's Book.	*handout*
Closing: Ask participants: "How do you feel today?" Group answers with the koosh ball.	*koosh ball*
Evaluation: Ask participants: "How did you feel in class?" Participants point to a face representing how they felt.	

Love is the foundation of dialog.

3. Crossing the Border

Theme: Immigration

Language Objectives

✎ be able to tell a story in the present and past tense

✎ be able to talk about coming to the U.S.

Code

Trabajaba en el campo con mi familia en México. Oí decir que aquí en los Estados Unidos puedes ganar mucho. Vine mojado. Me costó mucho. Quise cruzar el desierto. Tomó cuatro días caminando. Pero la "migra" nos agarró. Nos tomaron fotos. Nos hicieron muchas preguntas y nos regresaron a México. Intentamos otra vez pero no agarraron de nuveo. Esta vez tuvimos que pasar la noche en la carcél con otras cien personas. Por fin llegamos. Crucé el desierto con 50 personas. Me fuí a Nueva York donde vive mi hermano. Quince días después encontré trabajo como lavaplatos. Tengo un año de estar aquí.

Story

Read the story about crossing the border. Look at the questions for dialog to initiate a dialog about the story.

Questions for Dialog

1. Describe

What happens in the story?

Who is the story about?

2. Interpret and Relate

What do we call a person who leaves their country to live in another country?

Where do immigrants come from when they come to the U.S.?

How are immigrants treated in the U.S.?

Why do immigrants come to the U.S.? Why did you come to the U.S.?

3. Analyze and Act

What economic and cultural contributions do immigrants make to the U.S.?

Why are immigrants often treated poorly in this country?

Why are the wages immigrants earn so low?

What can we do to make sure immigrants are treated with dignity and respect?

Activities	Materials
Warm-Up: Error Correction: Write "My name _____" and "I from _____" on the board. Invite group to correct mistakes.	
Code: Facilitate a discussion about the story on p. 24 using the questions for dialog as a guide.	*story*
Speaking & Listening *Activity #1: LEA Picture Story* 1. Invite participants to talk about experiences coming here. 2. Choose one of the stories to study in class. 3. Translate the story from Spanish into English. 4. Participants illustrate parts of the story. 5. Collect the illustrations. 6. Talk about the illustrations in English. *Activity #2: Sequencing Activity* 1. Pass out the illustrations to the group. 2. Participants practice telling parts of the story in English. 3. Put the illustrations in sequence on the board. 4. Practice telling the whole story in English. *Option: Crossing the Border* If the discussion about the code doesn't generate a story from the group, study the story on p.25 of the Student's Book.	*butcher paper* *markers*
Break	
Reading & Writing *Activity #1: Matching Game* 1. Write a sentence next to each illustration on the board. 2. Read the sentences chorally. 3. Participants copy sentences of the story onto tagboard. 4. Participants practice reading their parts of the story. 5. Play matching game with pictures and sentences. *Activity #2: Grammar Exercise* 1. Group helps you circle the verbs of the story on the board. 2. Erase the rest of the story. 3. Introduce the present tense of those verbs and write them on the board. 4. Participants copy present/past tense of verbs onto index cards. 5. Play matching game with index cards.	*tagboard* *index cards*
Closing: Participants practice telling the story in English.	
Evaluation: Ball toss: Participants pass the ball and say one thing that they learned in today's class.	*koosh ball*

Notes

Looking for Work

Theme: Neoliberalism

Content

A Daily Wage

Day Labor Jobs

Negotiating a Job

Info. about our Employers

Unit Goal

The purpose of this unit is to study how neoliberalism has affected Latin America and Latinos in the U.S. As a part of our study, we will brainstorm alternatives to the neoliberal model and consider how to confront this ideology as a community.

Note: For more information on neoliberalism, see: 10 Plagas de Globalizacion Neoliberal, Asociacion Equipo Maiz, San Salvador, 1999.

1. Earning a Daily Wage

Theme: Neoliberalism

Language Objectives

- ✎ be able to recognize and say the names for the bills and coins
- ✎ be able to count money
- ✎ be able to read and write wages for day labor jobs

Vocabulary

- ✍ one dollar, five dollars, ten dollars, twenty dollars, etc.

Code

Questions for Dialog

1. Describe

What do we see in the picture?
What are the people doing?
How much is the employer offering?

2. Interpret and Relate

Do you think the wage agreed on is a fair wage?
Why is the person in the picture willing to work for so little?
Why does the employer hire someone for so little?
What is the legal minimum wage in our state?
Have you ever been in a situation like this?

3. Analyze and Act

What can the workers in the picture do to prevent this situation from taking place?
What can we do as a group to fight for fair wages when we do day labor?

Activities	Materials
Warm-Up: Form a circle and do a chain drill with the group: "I am from _____ and he/she is from _____."	*koosh ball*
Code: Facilitate a discussion about the drawing on p.28 using the questions for dialog as a guide.	*drawing*
Speaking & Listening *Activity #1: Wages Circle Toss* 1. Ask: "How much do you earn when you do day labor?" 2. Write the wages on the board (i.e. $9/hr), then point to the wages, and ask: "How much?" 3. Go through prepared wage flashcards asking: "How much?" 4. Show pictures of jobs and ask: "How much for painting?" 5. Pass out flashcards and practice saying the wages.	*job pictures* *flashcards*
Activity #2: Koosh Ball 1. Hold up a dollar bill and ask: "How much?" 2. Group practices saying the amounts of all the bills. 3. Repeat with coins.	*play money*
Activity #3: Counting Money 1. Count the money in your wallet and say: "I have _____." 2. Participants count their money. 3. Pass out different amounts of play money. 4. Participants count money and say: "I have _____."	
Break	
Reading & Writing *Activity #1: Writing Activity* 1. Tape the bills to the board. 2. Ask group to help you write amounts in numbers and in words. 3. Group reads through the list. 4. Repeat with coins.	*play money*
Activity #2: Matching Game 1. Tape the job pictures to the board. 2. Group helps you write the wages beside the pictures in numbers and in words. 3. Group reads through the wages. 4. Group copies wages onto tagboard. 5. Play matching game with the pictures and the wages.	*job pictures*
Closing: Game: Facilitator says a price. Teams write the numerical value for that price, or count out that amount.	*play money*
Evaluation: Draw happy, sad, and neutral faces on the board. Group members point to faces to evaluate class.	

Playing games promotes equality and participation.

2. Day Labor Jobs
Theme: Neoliberalism

Language Objectives
- be able to say and write different kinds of day labor jobs
- be able to conjugate the verb "to be"

Vocabulary
- painter, roofer, landscaper, mover, etc.

Code

Questions for Dialog

1. Describe
What do you see in this picture?
Who is the man in the tie? What is he thinking about?
Who is the man in the tie talking to? Who are the other people in the picture?

2. Interpret and Relate
How much do you think the boss earns?
How much do you think the workers earn?
Why do you think the difference in salary is so great?
Have you noticed this kind of disparity in Central America? What about in the U.S.?

3. Analyze and Act
If our work is so difficult, why are we paid so little?
What can we do to fight for fair wages for the work that we do?
What can we do to change the conditions that cause this kind of economic injustice?

Activities	Materials
Warm-Up: Practice names and greetings: "My name is _____. How are you?" When group is comfortable, generate other greetings.	*koosh ball*
Code: Facilitate a discussion about the drawing on p. 30 using the questions for dialog as a guide.	*drawing*
Speaking & Listening *Activity #1: Picture Activity* 1. Say: "I'm a teacher." 2. Show pictures of day labor jobs, point to the picture, and say: "He/She is a _____." 3. Point to the pictures again and ask: "What's his/her job?" Group responds: "He's/She's a _____." 4. Divide the class into groups of two. Pass out pictures to each group. 5. Pairs practice asking and answering questions about the pictures. *Activity #2: Line-up* 1. Pass out pictures. 2. Participants line-up according to what job: ☞ pays the most/least ☞ is the most/least difficult ☞ is the most/least dangerous	*pictures* *pictures*
Break	
Reading & Writing *Activity #1: Cloze* 1. Tape job pictures to the board and ask group to help you write the names of the jobs next to the pictures. 2. Ask participants to copy names of jobs onto tagboard. 3. Participants practice reading their tagboard. 4. Review uses of the verb "to be." 5. Write on board: "I am a _____." and "We are _____." 6. Participants take turns filling in blanks with tagboard. 7. Now write: "He is a _____." and "She is a _____." 8. Fill in blanks with tagboard. *Activity #2: Cloze* 1. Group helps you write short dialog on the board: Employer: I need a _____. Worker: I'm a _____. 2. Hold up one of the pictures and say: "I need a _____." 3. Participants find tagboard to complete the sentence.	*tagboard* *pictures* *tagboard*
Closing: What other kinds of jobs are there? What jobs pay the most? Which ones pay the least?	
Evaluation: Discussion: Was the class useful? What other aspects of employment would the group like to learn about?	

As educators we are polititians; we engage in political acts.

3. Negotiating a Job on the Street

Theme: Neoliberalism

Language Objectives

- ✎ be able to negotiate a job in a day labor situation
- ✎ be able to evaluate day labor working conditions

Vocabulary

- ✍ How much do you pay? Can you pay more? What kind of work? etc.

Code

Questions for Dialog

1. Describe

What do we see in this picture?
What are the people doing?
Does anyone know this place or a place like it?

2. Interpret and Relate

Who are the people waiting for work here? Who are the employers?
What do you think the wages and working conditions are like in this place?
Have you ever looked for work here or in a place like it?

3. Analyze and Act

Why do you think places like this one exist?
What economic conditions force us to come so far from our homes to look for work?
What do you think are the causes of these economic conditions?
What can we do to fight for fair wages and better working conditions in places like the one in the picture?

Activities	Materials
Warm-up: With the koosh ball, practice: "My name is _____. I am from_____." When group is comfortable, add: "I need a job."	*koosh ball*
Code: Facilitate a discussion about the photograph on p. 32 using the questions for dialog as a guide.	*photograph*
Speaking & Listening *Activity #1: Brainstorm* 1. Brainstorm a list of questions that workers need to ask employers when negotiating a day labor job. 2. Ask the group to help you translate the first question into English. 3. Brainstorm possible responses to the question. 4. Practice asking and answering question with koosh ball. 5. Repeat with other questions. *Activity #2: Role Play* 1. Based on questions, construct a dialog between worker and employer. 2. Demonstrate the dialog. 3. Invite volunteers to play the role of the worker. 4. Experiment with variations on the dialog.	*koosh ball*
Break	
Reading & Writing *Activity #1: Worksheet* 1. Participants fill in the worksheet on p. 35 of the Student's Book. 2. Group evaluates employers' answers on the worksheet. 3. Participants circle "OK" or "NO GOOD" based on their evaluation. *Activity #2: Question Pile* 1. Ask participants to write questions onto tagboard. 2. Group reads the questions chorally. 3. Shuffle the questions. 4. Volunteers draw questions and practice answering them.	*handout* *tagboard*
Closing: Divide class into a group of employers and a group of workers. Groups ask and answer questions.	
Evaluation: Write lesson activities on the board. Students say if they thought each part was "GOOD", "OK", or "NO GOOD".	

Democracy is made through reflection and practice.

. . . .

4. Getting Information About our Employers

Theme: Neoliberalism

Language Objectives

✎ be able to give and ask for personal information

Vocabulary

✍ What's your name? What's your last name? What's your address? What's your phone number? Do you have a business card? etc.

Code

Skit

Do a skit of a day laborer complaining to a friend about how his/her employer didn't pay the promised wage. Look at the questions for dialog and brainstorm solutions.

Questions for Dialog

1. Describe

What did we see in the skit?
Who are the characters? What are they doing?
How do you think the characters in the skit feel?
What else did you notice about the skit?

2. Interpret and Relate

Why do you think the employer doesn't pay the worker?
What could the worker in the skit have done to protect himself?
Have you ever been in this situation? What happened?

3. Analyze and Act

What can a worker do to protect himself when he does day labor?
What can we do as a group to improve the working conditions of day laborers?
How can we improve conditions locally, regionally, and nationally?

Activities	Materials
Warm-Up: Review the alphabet. Practice saying: "How do you spell that?" Participants take turns spelling their names.	
Code: Facilitate a discussion about the skit using the questions for dialog as a guide.	
Speaking & Listening *Activity #1: Getting Info. from your Employer* 1. Write your personal information on the board. (Juan Hernandez; 1283 T St NW etc.) 2. Point to your name and say: "Name", then point to your address and say: "Address", etc. 3. Group practices saying the new vocabulary chorally. 4. Elicit ways to ask for information. (What is your name?) 5. Pair up and practice asking and answering the questions. *Activity #2: Role Play* 1. Role play a dialog between a day laborer who is asking his employer for his personal information. 2. Model the dialog with puppets or pictures. 3. Invite a volunteer to play the role of the day laborer. 4. Invite a volunteer to play the role of the employer.	
Break	
Reading & Writing *Activity #1: Information Grid* 1. Make an information grid on the board similar to the one on p.36 of the Student's Book. 2. Ask for the students' personal info. and fill it into the grid. 3. Participants ask each other for their personal info. and fill it into in the grid. 4. Participants fill in the worksheet on p. 36 by circulating around the room asking each other for personal info. *Activity #2: Question Pile* 1. Ask group to help you write the personal information questions on the board. (What is your name?, etc.) 2. Participants write the questions onto tagboard. 3. Group reads the questions, in pairs, and individually. 4. Group draws and answers questions from a question pile.	*handout* *tagboard*
Closing: Bingo: Fill in bingo sheets with new vocabulary. Say: "What is your name." Participants cross out "Name."	*bingo sheets*
Evaluation: Participants pass the koosh ball and say one thing that they learned in class today.	*koosh ball*

Notes

Where we Work

Theme: The Transformative Power of Work

Content

Working Verbs

Tools (day 1)

Tools (day 2)

Telling Time

Unit Goal

The work we do impacts us as individuals, it impacts our community, and it impacts the local and national economies of the U.S. and Latin America. In this unit, we will study the power of our work to transform us. We will analyze the economic contributions of day laborers and we will brainstorm ways to improve working conditions for Latinos.

1. Working Verbs
Theme: The Transformative Power of Work

Learning Objectives

✎ be able to use the present continuous to talk about work

Vocabulary

✍ painting, raking leaves, breaking concrete, hammering, etc.

Code

Puzzle

Create a puzzle with the words "*Work with dignity for women and men.*" Lay the puzzle pieces on the table and invite the group to put it together. Use the questions fo dialog to talk about the puzzle.

Questions for Dialog

1. Describe

What do we see in the puzzle?
What does the puzzle say?

2. Interpret and Relate

What do you think the statement means?
What kind of work "dignifies" us?
What kind of work make us feel bad?
How else does our work affect us?

3. Analyze and Act

What can we do as a group to improve our working conditions?
What can we do to ensure that day laborers are treated with respect at work?
What else can we do to address this problem?

Activities	Materials
Warm-Up: Koosh ball activity: "How long have you been here?" "I've been here _____ years."	*koosh ball*
Code: Facilitate a discussion about the puzzle using the questions for dialog as a guide.	*puzzle*
Speaking & Listening *Activity #1: TPR* 1. Pantomime a day labor action and say: I am _____. 2. Group pantomimes that action and says: I am _____. 3. Generate other actions day laborers do at work. 4. Group pantomimes the actions and says the verbs. 5. Explain uses of the present continuous. *Activity #2: Slapjack* 1. Show pictures of day laborers working. 2. Point to the picture and say: He/She is _____. 3. Pass out pictures. 4. Group holds up pictures and say: He/She is _____. 5. Collect the cards, lay them on the table and say: "Which one is _____?" 6. Play slap jack with the pictures.	*pictures*
Break	
Reading & Writing *Activity #1: Sentence Scramble* 1. Tape the pictures one by one on the board. 2. Group helps you write sentences for each of the pictures. 3. Make flashcards for each word in 3-4 of the sentences. 4. Collect the cards and scramble the sentences. 5. Participants arrange the sentences in small groups. 6. Create question flashcards. (What is he doing?) 7. Repeat. *Activity #2: Role Play* 1. Role play a dialog between worker and employer with the worker asking: "What are we doing today?" 2. Group helps you write out the conversation on the board. 3. Practice reading the conversation chorally and in pairs. *Activity #3: To Do List* 1. Make a To Do list with the verbs. 2. Participants take turns giving instructions on their lists.	*paper for flashcards*
Closing: Pantomime actions and ask: "What am I doing?"	
Evaluation: Invite participants to draw faces on the board representing how they felt in class today.	

Popular Education should promote a consiousness of gender, respect for human rights and environment.

2. Tools (day 1)

Theme: The Transformative Power of Work

Language Objectives.

- be able to give and follow instructions at work
- be able to ask for the location of an object

Vocabulary

- names of common tools used by day laborers

Code

Questions for Dialog

1. Describe

What do we see in the picture?
What kind of work is the person in the picture doing?
What is he building?

2. Interpret and Relate

How do you think the structure the worker is building will be used?
Who will use it? What will be the affect on the person who uses it?
What is the affect on the person who built it?
Have you ever done this kind of work?

3. Analyze and Act

How does the work that we do transform the world around us?
Who benefits from the work that we do?
How does our work affect the local, regional, and national economy?
What can we do to teach others about our work?

Activities	Materials
Warm-Up: Ball toss: "What's this called in English?" "How do you say _____ in English?"	*koosh ball*
Code: Facilitate a discussion about the photograph on p.40 using the questions for dialog as a guide.	*picture*
Speaking & Listening *Activity #1: Ball Toss* 1. Ask the group to choose the kind of work it wants to study. 2. Invite participants to draw pictures of tools from that kind of work onto index cards. 3. Form a circle and do a ball toss activity with pictures. *Activity #2: TPR* 1. Facilitator leads TPR activity with the tools. 2. Group practices following and giving instructions: Pick it up. Put it away Put it down. Put it in the truck. Give it to _____. Where's the _____? 3. With the tools on the table, group practices giving and following instructions: Can you get me the _____? Can you give _____ the _____? Can you put the _____ in the truck?	*index cards* *koosh ball*
Break	
Reading & Writing *Activity #1: Matching Game* 1. Tape the pictures of the tools onto the board. 2. Invite the group to help you spell the names of the tools. 3. Point to the words and say the vocabulary. 4. Participants copy vocabulary words onto index cards. 5. Play matching game with tools and pictures. *Activity #2: Worksheet* 1. Guide participants through the worksheet on p.42 of the Student's Book.	*index cards* *handout*
Closing: Form a circle with tools. A player throws ball in air and says a tool. Player with that tool has to catch ball.	*koosh ball*
Evaluation: Discuss how the participants liked the class. What did they like? What didn't they like?	*handout*

The role of the teacher is not to impart knowledge, but to participate with the group in the creation of knowledge.

3. Tools (day 2)

Theme: The Transformative Power of Work

Language Objectives

✎ be able to say where an object is located

Vocabulary

✍ common tools used by day laborers

✍ on top of, next to, under, across from, in, etc.

Code

Questions for Dialog

1. Describe

What do we see in the picture?
What is the worker in the picture doing? What is he building?
What is he holding in his hand?

2. Interpret and Relate

How do you think the structure the worker is building will be used?
Who will use it? How will it affect the person who uses it?
How does building the structure affect the worker?
Have you ever done this kind of work?

3. Analyze and Act

How does the work we do transform us?
Who benefits from the work we do? How do they benefit?
What can we teach others about the benefits of our work?

Activities	Materials
Warm-Up: Do TPR activity with common actions such as Come, Go, Stand Up, Sit Down, etc. Higher level participants take turns leading the group.	
Code: Facilitate a discussion about the picture using the questions for dialog as a guide.	*picture*
Speaking & Listening *Activity #1: Vocabulary* 1. Ask the group to choose the kind of work it wants to study. 2. Invite group to draw pictures of tools onto index cards. 3. Participants hold up cards, and facilitator asks: "What's this called?" 4. Ball toss with new vocabulary. *Activity #2: Prepositions of Location* 1. Place one of the tools in some relation to an object and says how it relates to that object. "The hammer is next to the saw", for example. 2. Group repeats sentences chorally. 3. Now place a tool on the table and ask: "Where's the ____? 4. Repeat with different locations. 5. Change the location of the tool and ask where it is. 6. Practice in pairs.	*index cards* *tools*
Break	
Reading & Writing *Activity #1: Bingo* 1. Group helps you write the names of the tools on the board. 2. Point to the words and read through the tools. 3. Participants copy tools onto bingo sheets. 4. Play bingo with new vocabulary. *Activity #2: Tic Tac Toe* 1. Tape one of the bingo sheets to the wall. 2. Group divides into two teams. 3. Play Tic Tac Toe: Teams ask each other: "Where's the _____?" 4. Teams answer using prepositions: "It's next to the ____."	*bingo sheets*
Closing: Ball Toss: Review the names of the tools in English.	*koosh ball*
Evaluation: Pass out index cards. Participants write: GOOD, OK, or No GOOD, depending on how they like the class.	*index cards*

Dialog cannot exist without humility.

4. What Time Tomorrow?

Theme: The Transformative Power of Work

Language Objectives

✎ be able to ask for and give the time
✎ be able to read and write the time

Vocabulary

✍ What time is it? It's _____. What time tomorrow? I'll pick you up at 7:30.

Code

Questions for Dialog

1. Describe

What do we see in the picture?
How do the workers in the picture look? How do you think they feel?
What kind of work do they do?

2. Interpret and Relate

How do we feel when we are working steadily?
How do we feel physically? Mentally? Emotionally?
How do we feel when we are not working?

3. Analyze and Act

How does our work affect us then? Does it change us? If so, how?
How do we transform our community through our work?
Does our work have a positive or a negative impact on us personally?
Does our work have a positive or a negative impact on our community?

Activities	Materials
Warm-Up: Practice the numbers chorally 1-20. Form a circle and play Hot Potato. Repeat with numbers by 10's through 100.	*koosh ball*
Code: Facilitate a discussion about the photograph on p.44 using the questions for dialog as a guide.	*picture*
Speaking & Listening *Activity #1: Clock Activity* 1. Point to a play clock and ask: "What time is it?" 2. Draw a clock on the board, set the clock to different times asking: "What time is it now?" 3. Group practices with digital and analog time. 4. Pass out play clocks to pairs (see p. 47 of Student's Book). 5. Pairs practice asking each other: "What time is it?" *Activity #2: Mini Dialogs* 1. Role play a short conversation between an employer and a day laborer asking for times. Day Labor: "What time tomorrow?" Employer: "I'll pick you up at 7:00." 2. Model the dialog with puppets or pictures. 3. Invite volunteers to play the role of the day laborer. 4. Pair up and practice the dialog. 5. Repeat with another conversation.	*pictures* *play clocks*
Break	
Reading & Writing *Activity #1: Writing the Times* 1. Tape the play clocks to the board. 2. Ask group to help you write out the times. 3. Point to the times and read the words. 4. Participants take turns reading the times. 5. Copy the times onto tagboard for next activity. *Activity #2: Cloze* 1. Ask the group to help you write out one of the dialogs from the earlier activity. 2. Read the dialog chorally and in pairs. 3. Erase the times in the dialog. 4. Say the dialog again. 5. Participants complete the sentence with tagboard.	*tagboard*
Closing: Review times using play clocks and the koosh ball.	*play clocks* *koosh ball*
Evaluation: Participants pass the ball saying one thing that they learned in class today.	*koosh ball*

Notes

Getting an Education

Theme: Popular Education

Content

Work Experience

Job Skills

English Class

Unit Goal

Popular education involves identifying and valuing the skills, knowledge and experience gained informally. This is the theme of our study in unit five. In addition, we will search for strategies to continue the process of lifelong learning.

1. Work Experience

Theme: Popular Education

Language Objectives

- ✎ be able to talk about work experience
- ✎ identify the verb "to be" in the present and past tense

Vocabulary

- ✍ painter, carpenter, roofer, mechanic, etc.

Code

Questions for Dialog

1. Describe

What do you see in the picture?
What are the people doing?
What do you think they are saying?

2. Interpret and Relate

What is education?
What is the difference between formal and informal education?
What experiences do we have with formal education?
What experiences have we gained informally?

3. Analyze and Act

What circumstances prevented us from going to school?
Does it mean we don't have an education if we didn't go to school?
What benefits can we obtain by participating in educational programs?
What skills and experience do we have that we can share with others?

Activities	Materials
Warm-Up: Review "What's your name? Where are you from?" When group feels comfortable, add: "Where do you live?"	*koosh ball*
Code: Facilitate a discussion about the photograph on p.48 using the questions for dialog as a guide.	*picture*
Listening & Speaking *Activity #1: Pictures of Jobs* 1. Draw a picture of your job on the board and say: "Now I'm a _____." Participants say their jobs. 2. Draw a picture of a job you had before and say: "Before I was a _____." Participants say jobs they used to have. 3. Participants draw pictures of a job they have now and a job they had before on two index cards. 4. Participants write their names on the cards. 5. Participants present cards to each other and the group. *Activity #2: Job Pile* 1. Collect cards and divide into two piles. 2. Draw one of the cards in the now pile and read the picture. For example: "Luis is a painter." 3. Participants draw cards in the "now" pile. 4. Repeat with the "before" pile.	*index cards* *markers*
Break	
Reading & Writing *Activity #1: Writing the Jobs* 1. Generate the spelling of the jobs on the cards. 2. Participants help you write the jobs on the board. 3. Participants write their jobs on the back of their cards. 4. Practice reading the jobs. *Activity #2: Cloze* 1. Write "In Maryland I am a _____." and "In my country I was a _____." on the board. 2. Participants fill in the blanks with their pictures and the vocabulary words on the backs of their cards. 3. Review the verb "to be" in the present and past tense.	
Closing: Participants work on p. 54 from the Student's Book.	
Evaluation: Form a human train. Participants stop the train (by yelling "Stop!") to respond to the evaluation questions.	

True dialog cannot exist unless the dialogers engage in critical thinking.

2. Job Skills

Theme: Popular Education

Language Objectives

- ✎ be able to talk about job skills
- ✎ What can you do? I can.../I can't...

Vocabulary

- ✍ carpentry, roofing, construction, painting, landscaping, etc.

Code

Questions for Dialog

1. Describe

What do we see in the picture?
What kind of work is the worker doing?

2. Interpret and Relate

What skills does he have to do this work?
Where do you think he learned these skills?
Do you think he learned them in a formal or an informal setting?
What job skills do we possess?
How did we acquire our skills?

3. Analyze and Act

What can we do to gain more job skills?
What skills do we have that we can share with others?
What else can we do to further our education in general?

Activities	Materials
Warm-Up: Talk about food that you like. Practice: "I like _____." "I don't like _____."	*koosh ball*
Code: Facilitate a discussion about the photograph on p.50 using the questions for dialog as a guide.	*photograph*
Speaking & Listening *Activity #1: New Vocabulary* 1. Hold up pictures of common day labor jobs. 2. Model job skills: "I can do carpentry work." 3. Ask participants to say what they can do. 4. Using the pictures, introduce the question: "Can you do _____work?" 5. Participants respond saying: "Yes, I can." or "No, I can't." 6. Participants say what they *can* and *can't* do. *Activity #2: Information Grid* 1. Create an information grid on the board. 2. Tape the pictures of day labor jobs into the grid. 3. Make a check mark in the grid based on what you *can* and *can't* do. 4. Repeat process with class participants. 5. Participants practice asking and answering questions using the grid.	*pictures*
Break	
Reading & Writing *Activity #1: TPR* 1. Pass out two index cards to each class participant. 2. Participants write "Yes, I can" on one card and "No, I can't" on the other. 3. Ask participants: "Can you do _____?" 4. Participants hold up the card to answer question. *Activity #2: Worksheet* 1. Guide group through the worksheet on p. 55 of the Student's Book.	*index cards* *handout*
Closing: Divide class into small groups and play the game on p.59 of the Student's Book.	*handout*
Evaluation: Elicit class activities. Using a colored marker, participants put a dot next to the activities they liked best.	*butcher paper* *markers*

3. English Class: Learning from Each Other

Theme: Popular Education

Language Objectives

- be able to express needs
- be able to ask for clarification: "Please repeat."

Vocabulary

- work experience, job skills, tools, safety equipment, etc.

Code

Song

Find the song *La Frasesita* by Los Jornaleros del Norte on the Internet. Listen to the song and start a dialog about it using the questions for dialog as a guide. (If you can't find the song, initiate a dialog about how it feels not to be able to speak English at work.)

Questions for Dialog

1. Describe

What do you hear in the song?
What is the song about?
How does the worker feel about having to learn English?
What else do you notice about the song?

2. Interpret and Relate

How is the worker treated by his boss?
Why do you think his boss treats him this way?
Have you ever been treated this way at work?

3. Analyze and Act

How does not speaking English affect us in this country?
What strategies can we use to make learning English easier?
What other ways can we work to further our education in general?

Activities	Materials
Warm-Up: Practice clarification language: "I don't understand." "Can you repeat that?" etc. Make a clarification language chart and put it on the wall.	*butcher paper* *markers*
Code: Facilitate a discussion about the song using the questions for dialog as a guide.	*song*
Speaking & Listening *Activity #1: Identifying Needs* 1. Show pictures of day laborers in different situations. 2. Group talks about the pictures. 3. Ask group: "When does he/she need English?" 4. Group makes suggestions. 5. Now facilitator asks group: "When do you need English?" 6. Group practices saying: "I need English _____." *Activity #2: Assessment/Evaluation* 1. Discuss the content of the employment lessons you have studied in the last weeks and tape corresponding pictures to the board: What is the most important? Is there anything missing that should be included? (If so, create another picture on butcher paper.) 2. Pass out 3-4 stickers to participants. 3. Participants place stickers on most important themes. 4. Discuss results.	*pictures* *koosh ball* *pictures*
Break	
Reading & Writing *Activity #1: Class Story* 1. Read the story on p.49 of the Student's Book while group follows along. 2. Pass out tagboard. Participants copy story onto tagboard. 3. Group reads sentences one at a time. 4. Collect the sentences and shuffle. 5. Participants put sentences in sequence. 6. Group reads story again. *Activity #2: Worksheet* 1. Guide participants in completing the worksheet on p. 56 of the Student's Book.	*story* *handout*
Closing: Koosh ball activity: Class participants take turns saying when they need English.	*koosh ball*
Evaluation: Discussion about the curriculum. What themes does the group like? What does it want to change?	

With popular education, the teachers learn and the learners teach.

Notes

Where we Live

Theme: Strengthening Community

Content

Unit Goal

Improving our social and economic welfare depends largely on the strength of our community. In this unit, we will discuss ways to increase the level of political and economic power of the Latino community both locally and nationally. We will also identify obstacles that impede us from participating more actively in our communities.

1. Asking for Directions
Theme: Strengthening Community

Language Objectives

✎ be able to give and follow directions

✎ be able to ask about location: "Where's the _____?"

Vocabulary

✍ left, right, turn right, turn left, turn around, go straight, etc.

Code

Questions for Dialog

1. Describe

What do we see in the picture?
Who are the people in the picture?
Does anyone recognize the place the people are standing?

2. Interpret and Relate

What is our community?
What are some important places in our community?
What people live and work in our community?
Where do you live and work?
Do you feel like a member of this community? Why? Why not?

3. Analyze and Act

What can we do to better acquaint ourselves with our communities?
How can we work for greater access to justice for Latinos in our communities?

Activities	Materials
Warm-Up: Review different ways of saying goodbye in English. Practice chorally and in pairs, then role play saying goodbye at work.	*koosh ball*
Code: Facilitate a discussion about the photograph on p.56 using the questions for dialog as a guide.	*photograph*
Speaking & Listening *Activity #1: TPR* 1. Do TPR activity with directions: Left, Right, etc. 2. Invite volunteers to give directions. *Activity #2: Chair Activity* 1. Set up two chairs several feet apart, sit down in one of the chairs, and direct yourself to the other chair. 2. Ask: "Where's the chair?" Invite group to direct you back. 3. Participants direct each other. 4. Try this activity using a blindfold. *Activity #3: Race* 1. Ask group members to pair up. 2. Set up a row of chairs at opposite end of the room. 3. One participant is the robot (eyes closed), the other gives directions. 4. The first pair to sit down in their chair is the winner. 5. Switch roles.	*blindfold*
Break	
Reading & Writing *Activity #1: Vocabulary* 1. Draw the directional symbols on board. 2. Ask participants to help you write the words beside the symbols. 3. Practice reading the new vocabulary. *Activity #2: Maze* 1. Create a maze with masking tape on the floor. 2. Brainstorm landmarks and copy them onto index cards. 3. Place landmarks on map. 4. Participants take turns directing each other to landmarks.	*tape* *markers* *index cards*
Closing: Tic Tac Toe: Put names of landmarks in the squares. Players take turns directing each other to the landmarks	
Evaluation: Write the language objectives on the board. Ask group if it feels like the objectives were met. Why? Why not?	

Think about the respect we owe to our learners' cultural identity.

2. Getting to Know our Neighborhood

Theme: Strengthening Community

Language Objectives

- be able to give and follow directions using a map
- be able to use adjectives to describe the neighborhood

Vocabulary

- bus stop, supermarket, gas station, restaurant, etc.

Code

Questions for Dialog

1. Describe

What do we see on the map?
What streets do we see on the map?
What are some of the places on the map?

2. Interpret and Relate

Does anyone know where the place is?
Who are the people who come to this place?
Who are some of the leaders and role models of this place?
What makes them leaders and role models of our community?

3. Analyze and Act

How much influence do our community leaders have politically and economically in our state as compared with other groups?
What can we do to increase the influence of Latino leaders regionally and nationally?
What can we do to develop our own leadership skills?

Activities	Materials
Warm-Up: Do TPR with directions: Go straight, turn left, turn right, turn around, come over here, go over there, etc.	
Code: Facilitate a discussion about the map on p.58 using the questions for dialog as a guide.	*map*
Speaking & Listening *Activity #1: Group Drawing* 1. Brainstorm landmarks in the neighborhood. 2. Draw a group map of the surrounding area. You might include streets, stores, parks, gas stations, bus stops, etc. 3. Use the koosh ball to allow everyone to participate. 4. Participants practice saying the words for what they draw. *Activity #2: Describing the Picture* 1. Introduce: "In our neighborhood there is/are...". 2. Point out difference between *hay* singular and *hay* plural. 3. Take turns describing the drawing. *Activity #3: Adjectives* 1. Add adjectives to describe the places on the map. 2. Ask, for example: "Is it a big store or a small store?" 3. Repeat with other places on the map. 4. Volunteers take turns describing the drawing.	*butcher paper* *markers*
Break	
Reading & Writing *Activity #1: Grammar Exercise* 1. Label the drawing of the neighborhood. 2. Practice reading the new words. 3. Now write a "There is..." column and a "There are..." column on the board 4. Participants write the places into the columns. *Activity #2: Group Story* 1. Have the group help you write about the drawing. 2. Read about the drawing as a class. 3. Read about the drawing in pairs. 4. Now erase some of the verbs. 5. Invite participants to fill in the blanks.	
Closing: Practice describing the place you live in your country. What are the similarities and differences?	
Evaluation: Lead a discussion: How is the class going? How can we make the class more participatory?	

The process of education creates new realities.

3. Taking the Bus
Theme: Strengthening Community

Language Objectives

- be able to understand basic directions
- be able to ask for information about public transportation

Vocabulary

- bus stop, bus pass, transfer, bus schedule, fare, peak fare, etc.
- Where can I catch the bus to Silver Spring? Take the _____.

Code

Skit

Do a skit about a day laborer having trouble reading a bus schedule and wondering why there aren't schedules published in languages other than English.

Questions for Dialog

1. Describe
What did we see in the skit?
What does the person in the skit need?
What happens at the end of the skit?

2. Interpret and Relate
Why can't the person in the skit get the information in Spanish?
Why is it so hard for us to get important documents we need in Spanish?
Have you ever had this problem?

3. Analyze and Act
What other documents would we like to see published in our native language?
What can we do to ensure access to documents in our own language?
What else can we do to as a group to promote language rights in our state?

Activities	Materials
Warm-Up: Review times: Pass out play clocks. Participants circulate around the room asking: "What time is it?"	*play clocks*
Code: Facilitate a discussion about the skit using the questions for dialog as a guide.	
Speaking & Listening *Activity #1: New Vocabulary* 1. Hold up a bus pass and ask: "What's this called?" 2. Repeat with transfer, bus schedule, and flashcards of peak fare, off-peak fare, peak hours, and off-peak hours. 3. Group practices new vocabulary. 4. Pass out items. Participants hold up and say chorally. 5. Say: "How do you ask for something in English?" 6. Practice making requests: "I need a _____." *Activity #2: Information Grid* 1. Ask the group: "What bus do you take?" 2. Fill in names and bus numbers on an information grid. 3. Add bus stop location, destination, and times. 4. Use the grid to talk about taking the bus: "I take the #15 from Langley Park to Silver Spring." 5. Practice with the koosh ball.	*bus pass* *bus schedule* *transfer* *hours* *fares* *koosh ball*
Break	
Reading & Writing *Activity #1: Reading a Bus Schedule* 1. Pass out bus schedules. 2. Practice reading the times on the schedule. 3. Teach the verbs: leaves, arrives, goes, etc. 4. Make sentences about the schedule: "The bus leaves Silver Spring at 7:00." *Activity #2: Worksheet* 1. Play bingo with the times on the bus schedule. Facilitator calls out the times.	*bus schedules* *bingo sheets*
Closing: Role play a dialog between a bus driver and some-one asking for directions.	
Evaluation: Evaluate the class orally using the koosh ball.	*koosh ball*

Banking education anesthetizes and inhibits creative power.

. . . .

4. Taking the Metro
Theme: Strengthening Community

Language Objectives

- be able to say and write the colors
- be able to ask for information about public transportation

Vocabulary

- red, black, blue, etc.

Code

Un día conseguí trabajo. Fue en Anacostia. Está lejos de aquí. Eramos tres. Era demolición. Al final del día el patrón nos dejó en Anacostia.

No hablemos inglés. No sabíamos como regresar. Finalmente le preguntamos a una mujer simpática. Le dijimos: "Where's Silver Spring?" Nos dijo tomen el metro. Regresamos pero tomó mucho tiempo.

Story

Read the story about a day laborer getting lost. Start a dialog about the story using the questions for dialog as a guide.

Questions for Dialog

1. Describe

What is the story about?
What happens to the workers in the story?
How does the story end?

2. Interpret and Relate

What do the workers do to get back to Silver Spring? What do they say?
Why does the employer leave them in Anacostia?
Has this ever happened to you?

3. Analyze and Act

How can we prevent this kind of thing from happening?
What is important to know when we are taking public transportation?
How can we learn more about public transportation and other resources in our community?

Activities	Materials
Warm-Up: Ball Toss: Practice clarification language: "Can you repeat that please?" "I don't understand." etc.	*koosh ball*
Code: Facilitate a discussion about the story on p.62 using the questions for dialog as a guide.	*story*
Speaking & Listening *Activity #1: TPR* 1. Show color flashcards and ask: "What color is this?" 2. Point to classroom objects and ask: "Is this blue or red?" 3. Do TPR with participants pointing to the colors. *Activity #2: Asking for Directions* 1. Draw a map of the Metro on the board using colored chalk. 2. Practice saying the different lines: "This is the red line." 3. Ask participants what Metro stops they know and write them on the map. 4. Ask: "What line goes to _____?" 5. Participants practice asking each other. *Activity #3: Asking for Directions* 1. Imagine that you are lost at one of the stations and need to get back to Silver Spring. What would you say? 2. Role play a person asking for directions. 3. Volunteers take the place of the person who is lost.	*flashcards* *colored chalk*
Break	
Reading & Writing *Activity #1: Writing Directions* 1. Invite the group to help you label the names of the lines. 2. Point to the lines and practice saying: "This is the red line." etc. 3. Ask for directions again and transcribe what the group says on the board. 4. Ask for help in making corrections. 5. Practice reading directions. 6. Repeat with other directions. *Activity #2: Worksheet* 1. Guide participants through the worksheet on p.69 of the Student's Book.	*handout*
Closing: Participants take turns leading each other through a Metro map on floor. Use colored string or tape for map.	*string or tape*
Evaluation: Participants pass the ball to music. When the music stops, player with the ball answers evaluation question.	*koosh ball*

Notes

Talking about Race

Theme: Struggle for Equality

Content

Describing People

Nationality

Race

Historical Struggle

Unit Goal

The purpose of this unit is to recognize and analyze racism and to consider how racism affects us. Through critical discussions involving race, we will confront our own prejudices as well as those of the larger society. We hope to reach a point in which we not only take pride in our own racial identity, but learn to respect others and become promoters of both racial and gender equality.

1. Talking about our Differences
Theme: Struggle for Equality

Language Objectives
- be able to describe someone physically
- the verb "to be"

Vocabulary
- tall, short, thin, old, young, light-skinned, dark-skinned, etc.
- black, brown, blond, straight, curly hair, etc.

Code

Skit

Do a skit about a woman who is pregnant being discriminated against when trying to get an apartment.

Questions for Dialog

1. Describe
What did we see in the skit?
What were the people in the skit doing?
What happens at the end of the skit?

2. Interpret and Relate
Why wasn't the woman able to get an apartment?
What is discrimination?
What are some different kinds of discrimination?
Have you ever experienced discrimination in your own life?

3. Analyze and Act
What can we do if we suspect we are being discriminated against?
What can we do to make sure women and men are treated as equals?
What can we as a group do to fight discrimination?

Activities	Materials
Warm-Up: Discuss this unit's theme. What does "the struggle for equality" mean? Talk about the objectives of the unit. Review the verb "to be." Conjugate "to be" on the board.	*koosh ball*
Code: Facilitate a discussion about the skit on p.66 using the questions for dialog as a guide.	
Speaking & Listening *Activity #1: Pictures* 1. Hold up pictures of people, and describe their physical traits. 2. Repeat, asking: "What does she/he look like?" 3. Generate target vocabulary from the pictures. 4. Pass out pictures to participants. 5. Group forms a circle. 6. Participants toss koosh ball, point to to their pictures and ask the others: "What does she/he look like?" *Activity #2: Describing your partner* 1. Divide class into groups of two. 2. Facilitator starts by describing his/her partner physically. 3. Participants describe their partners. 4. Facilitator says, *Vamos al Par!* and participants find another partner. Repeat a couple of times 5. New pairs take turns describing each other.	*pictures* *koosh ball*
Break	
Reading & Writing *Activity #1: Matching Game* 1. Tape the pictures to the board. 2. Ask the group to help you write sentences that describe the people in the pictures physically. 3. Group practices reading the sentences. 4. Group copies the sentences onto tagboard. 5. Students match the pictures with the tagboard. *Activity #2: Writing about your Partner* 1. Divide class into groups of two. 2. Facilitator models writing about his/her partner on the board. 3. Participants write sentences about their partners. 4. Volunteers read sentences aloud.	*tagboard* *paper* *pencils*
Closing: Facilitator describes person in the room physically without saying who that person is. Group guesses identity.	
Evaluation: Koosh ball evaluation: What did you like about today's class? What could we improve for the next class?	*koosh ball*

2. Talking about Race

Theme: Struggle for Equality

Language Objectives

- be able to describe someone based on his/her country and race
- the verb "to be"

Vocabulary

- African American, Latino, black, white, Asian, Middle-Eastern, etc.
- El Salvador, Guatemala, the United States, Vietnam, etc.

Code

Skit

Do a skit about a Latino worker, an African American worker, and their white boss exchanging racial slurs.

Questions for Dialog

1. Describe

What did we see in the skit?
What were the people in the skit doing?
What happens at the end of the skit?

2. Interpret and Relate

What does the Latino worker say about his African American co-worker?
What does the African American co-worker say?
What is racism?
Have you ever experienced racism in your own life?

3. Analyze and Act

What can we do to improve relations between African Americans and Latinos?
How can we best respect people from other races?
What can we as a group do to promote racial equality?

Activities	Materials
Warm-Up: Ball Toss: "I need a job." When the group feels comfortable, you can add other needs: "I need _____."	*koosh ball*
Code: Facilitate a discussion about the skit on p.68 using the questions for dialog as a guide.	
Speaking & Listening *Activity #1: Pictures* 1. Hold up pictures of people of different races asking, "Where is she from? Where are they from?" etc. 2. Pass out pictures to participants. 3. Participants ask each other about the pictures. 4. Ask participants: How are the people in the pictures different? How are they similar? *Activity #2: Information Grid* 1. Tape the pictures on the board and make an information grid with categories for country and race. 2. Ask participants to help you fill in the grid. 3. Using the koosh ball, ask questions about the grid. *Activity #3: Respectful Language* 1. Talk about respectful language for different groups. 2. Add respectful and not respectful categories to the grid.	*pictures*
Break	
Reading & Writing *Activity #1: LEA Story* 1. Talk about a time one of the participants heard someone use racist language. What happened? 2. Group writes the story into simple Spanish. 3. Group translates the story into simple English. 4. Group copies the story sentence by sentence onto tagboard. 5. Participants practice reading the story. *Activity #2: Cloze Activity* 1. Copy the entire story in English onto the board. 2. Erase important words in the story. 3. Invite participants to help you fill in the story. 4. Participants practice writing the entire story.	*tagboard*
Closing: Review countries and race using the pictures.	*koosh ball*
Evaluation: Discuss what we can do as a group the next time we hear someone use racist language.	

3. What is Prejudice?
Theme: Struggle for Equality

Language Objectives

- be able to describe someone's personality
- the verb "to be"

Vocabulary

- friendly, unfriendly, hardworking, lazy, smart, stupid, proud, messy, generous, shy, cool, nice, timid, etc.

Code

Questions for Dialog

1. Describe
What do we see in the picture?
What are the people in the picture doing?
How do you think the African American worker in the picture feels?

2. Interpret and Relate
What is prejudice?
Where does prejudice come from?
What kinds of prejudice do people have about Latinos?
What kinds of prejudice do people have about other racial groups?
Have you ever been discriminated against based on your race?

3. Analyze and Act
What can we do to combat prejudice in our community?
What can we do to change people's prejudices about Latinos ?
What else can we do as a group to solve this problem?

Activities	Materials
Warm-Up: Review material from the previous lesson. Hold up pictures of people of different races and say, for example: "She's African American."	*pictures*
Code: Facilitate a discussion about the drawing on p.70 using the questions for dialog as a guide.	*picture*
Speaking & Listening *Activity #1: Brainstorm* 1. Write the word "Prejudice/Prejuicio" on the board. 2. Below, tape the pictures of people from different races. 3. Brainstorm prejudices about each group. 4. Write down the adjectives participants come up with below each picture, first in Spanish, then in English. 5. Participants practice using the adjectives to talk about themselves: "I'm not _____." 6. Group uses adjectives to talk about pictures: "He isn't____."	*pictures* *koosh ball*
Activity #2: Brainstorm 1. Now brainstorm adjectives that contradict the stereotypes. 2. Participants use the new adjectives to talk about themselves: "I'm not _____. I'm _____." 3. Participants use the new adjectives to talk about pictures.	*pictures* *koosh ball*
Break	
Reading & Writing *Activity #1: Chain Drill* 1. Participants write an adjective that doesn't apply to them on one side of an index card and an adjective that does apply to them on the other side of the card. 2. Group forms a circle and holds up cards. 3. Participants toss ball and say, "I'm not _____ and he's not _____."	*index cards* *koosh ball*
Activity #2: Story 1. Facilitator reads the story on p.77 of the Student's Book. 2. Volunteers read the story and translate. 3. Participants underline the target vocabulary. 4. Review uses of the verb "to be" in the story. 5. Group does the true/false exercises.	*handout*
Closing: Participants take turns describing friends and family based on their personality.	
Evaluation: Lead a discussion: How is the class going? How can we make the class more participatory?	

Organizing is an educational process.

4. A People's History

Theme: Struggle for Equality

Language Objectives

- to be able to read a simple text about historical events
- to learn about the struggle for equality of African Americans
- to be able to use the simple past of a few irregular verbs

Vocabulary

- irregular verbs

Code

Questions for Dialog

1. Describe
What did we see in the picture?
What is happening in the picture?
Who are the people in the picture ?

2. Interpret and Relate
What is slavery?
What do we know about slavery here in the United States?
Who became slaves in the United States? Why?
How do you think it felt to be a slave?

3. Analyze and Act
What can we do to learn more about African American history?
What can we do to learn more about our own people's historical struggles?
What can we do to fight for equality for all racial groups?

Activities	Materials
Warm-Up: Hold up pictures of people of different races. Ask participants: "Where is she/he from?" Discuss possiblities.	*pictures*
Code: Facilitate a discussion about the drawing on p.72 using the questions for dialog as a guide.	*picture*
Speaking & Listening *Activity #1: Timeline* 1. Show pictures of African American history from the Student's Book. Ask participants questions about the pictures. 2. Divide the class into small groups. 3. Invite groups to paste pictures of African American history onto the historical timeline. 4. Review African American history. (You can also invite someone from the Day Labor Center to talk about African American history.) 5. Participants revise their timelines and practice talking about the pictures. *Activity #2: Timeline* 1. Ask the group about the history of Latin America. 2. Invite groups to make timelines of Latin American history. 3. Groups present their timelines to the class.	*timelines* *pictures* *glue stick* *timelines* *markers*
Break **Reading & Writing** *Activity #1: Timeline* 1. Invite participants to help you write sentences about the pictures in the African American timeline. 2. Practice reading the sentences about African American history. 3. Participants copy the sentences onto the timeline. 4. Take turns reading the story. *Activity #2: Timeline* 1. Repeat activity #1 with Latin American timelines.	
Closing: Pass out the pictures of African American history. Participants talk about the pictures.	*pictures*
Evaluation: Evaluate the class orally using the koosh ball.	*koosh ball*

The objective of popular education is the transformation of society.

. . . .

Notes

Defending our Rights

Theme: Immigrant Rights

Content

A Safe Workplace

The Police

Fair Payment

Tenants' Rights

Unit Goal

To protect ourselves from exploitation we need to know how to defend our rights. The purpose of unit eight is to study our rights. We will also try to establish a link between defending our rights and group empowerment.

1. The Right to a Safe Workplace

Theme: Immigrant Rights

Language Objectives

✎ be able to make requests: I need... I want.... Give me... etc.

Vocabulary

✍ hard hat, mask, ear plugs, gloves, respirator, eye protection, etc.

Code

Questions for Dialog

1. Describe

What do we see in the picture?
What is the person doing?
What kind of work is it?

2. Interpret and Relate

What is the worker worried about?
Whose responsibility is it to ensure safe conditions at work?
Have you ever been asked to work in unsafe conditions?
Have you ever been hurt at work?

3. Analyze and Act

What are our rights if we get hurt at work?
What are some ways to improve saftey conditions at work?
How can we learn more about our rights concerning safety at work?
How can we ask for safety equipment in English?

Activities	Materials
Warm-Up: Ball toss. Review occupations: "I'm a painter."	*koosh ball*
Code: Facilitate a discussion about the drawing using the questions for dialog as a guide.	*drawing*
Speaking & Listening *Activity #1: New Vocabulary* 1. Show pictures of safety equipment (see Student's Book). 2. Discuss what safety equipment is used in different jobs. 3. Point to a picture and ask: "What's this?" 4. Pass out pictures to students. Participants hold up pictures, and practice vocabulary. *Activity #2: Making a Request* 1. Now lay the pictures on the table. 2. Elicit how to make a request in English. 3. Practice one of the suggestions saying: "I need a _____" 4. Pick up that picture from the table. 5. Invite volunteers to make requests. *Activity #3: Dialog* 1. Model a short dialog between an employer and a worker with the employer wanting the worker to do something dangerous and the worker requesting safety equipment. 2. Invite volunteers toplay the role of the worker.	*pictures* *pictures*
Break	
Reading & Writing *Activity #1: Bingo* 1. Tape pictures of safety equipment to the board 2. Ask participants to help you spell vocabulary. 3. Have students write vocabulary onto bingo sheets. 4. Play bingo with the new vocabulary. *Activity #2: Cloze* 1. Write up a few ways of making requests. 2. Leave a blank to insert the vocabulary, such as: "Give me _____." 3. Drill the cloze activity with pictures and words. 4. Invite participants to drill each other. *Activity #3: Worksheet* 1. Guide the participants through the worksheet on p.87 of the Student's Book.	*bingo sheets* *handout*
Closing: Do a word dictation with the the new vocabulary.	
Evaluation: Pass the koosh ball and participants say one thing they learned today.	*koosh ball*

It is important to show students the beauty in the ethical struggle.

2. The Right to Fair Treatment by the Police

Theme: Immigrant Rights

Language Objectives

- be able to respond to common questions asked by the police
- be able to respond quickly to police commands

Vocabulary

- What's your name? Where are you from? Where do you live? Do you have ID? Do you have a green card? etc.

Code

Una vez por la mañana llegó la policía a 7-11. Habían como 40 personas esperando trabajo y como a las 10:00 de la mañana llegó la policía porque los comerciantes se quejaron y los policías dijeron que no querían ver a nadie en ese sector y que si no despejaban el lugar iban a ponerles ticket, arrestarlos o llamar a la migra. Entones Guadalupe salió a defender y le dijo a los policías que los trabajadores tenían autorizado un sector específico para poder estar esperando trabajo. Al final hubo un acuerdo de que las personas podían estar en un lugar mantener el orden y el lugar limpio.

Story

Read the story about the police coming to the day laborer corner. Start a dialog about the story using the questions for dialog as a guide.

Questions for Dialog

1. Describe

What happens in the story?
What do the police do?
What do the workers on the corner do?
How does the story end?

2. Interpret and Relate

What are our rights if we are questioned by the police?
What are our rights if we are arrested?
Have you ever had an experience with the police in this country?

3. Analyze and Act

Why is the police presence greater in our community than in some other communities?
How can we defend our rights when dealing with the police?
What can we do to develop a better relationship between day laborers and police?

Activities	Materials
Warm-Up: Do TPR to introduce common police commands: Stop!/Freeze!/Don't move!/Walk straight ahead!/Come over here!/Let's go!/Spread your legs!/Arms to the side!, etc.	
Code: Facilitate a discussion about the story on p.78 using the questions for dialog as a guide.	*story*
Speaking & Listening *Activity #1: Group Role Play* 1. Role play a dialog about a worker being interrogated by the police. 2. Review the dialog starting with the first question the police ask. 3. Brainstorm ways of responding to the question. (Discuss appropriate answers.) 4. Practice the responses with the koosh ball. 5. Divide the class into two groups facing each other. One side is the police, the other is the person being interrogated. 6. Invite sides to call out questions and answers. *Activity #2: Role Play* 1. Do the skit between a day laborer and the police again. 2. This time incorporate some of the responses the group came up with in the first activity. 3. Invite a volunteer to play the role of the day laborer. 4. Invite a volunteer to play the role of the police.	*koosh ball*
Break	
Reading & Writing *Activity #1: Question Pile* 1. Write out the questions the police ask on the board. 2. Point to the questions and read chorally. 3. Ask participants to copy the questions onto slips of paper. 4. Shuffle the papers and make a question pile. 5. As group answers the questions, write responses on the board. *Activity #2: Cloze* 1. Group helps you write out the dialog on the board. 2. Take turns reading the dialog. 3. Erase key words and invite participants to fill in the blanks.	*blank paper*
Closing: Repeat warm-up activity.	
Evaluation: What else helps us defend our rights when dealing with the police? How can we include this into the lesson?	

Problem-posing education is revolutionary futurity.

3. The Right to Fair Payment

Theme: Immigrant Rights

Language Objectives

- be able to request your full wages: "Give me _____."
- be able to identify and count money

Vocabulary

- numbers 1-100
- verbs: owe, give, promise, etc.

Code

Skit

Do a skit about a worker not getting paid the right amount and not knowing what to say in English to ask for the rest of his money. Start a dialog about the skit using the questions for dialog as a guide.

Questions for Dialog

1. Describe

What happens in the skit?
What does the employer do?
What does the worker do?
How does the skit end?

2. Interpret and Relate

Why does the employer pay less than he promised to pay?
How does the worker react when he receives less than he was promised?
What could he have said or done instead?

3. Analyze and Act

What can we do to protect ourselves when we do day labor?
How can we make sure that we get paid for our work?
What can we do to inform ourselves and others about our rights?

Activities	Materials
Warm-up: Review money. Point to bills and say the amount. Pass out money to students. Participants say how much they have.	*play money*
Code: Facilitate a discussion about the skit using the questions for dialog as a guide.	
Speaking & Listening *Activity #1: Brainstorm* 1. Ask: "What can we say in English if we don't get paid?" 2. Pass out play money. 3. Model one of the suggestions: "Give me _____." 4. Practice asking for money in pairs. *Activity #2: Game* 1. Invite 4-5 volunteers to play a game. 2. Pass out money to players clearly stating the amount. 3. Pass out money to one player and say an incorrect amount. 4. That player has to say: "Wait! You owe me _____." *Activity #3: Role Play* 1. Role play a dialog between an employer and a worker where the employer gives the worker the wrong amount. 2. Model the dialog with pictures or puppets. 3. Invite volunteers to play the role, first of the worker, and then of the employer.	*play money*
Break	
Reading & Writing *Activity #1: Sequencing Activity* 1. Group helps you write out the dialog from the previous activity. 2. Point to the words and read chorally and in pairs. 3. Each participant copies a sentence from the dialog onto tagboard. 4. Participants hold up tagboard and group reads sentences. 5. Shuffle the dialog and invite the group to sequence it. *Activity #2: Worksheet* 1. Guide students through worksheet on p. 84 of the Student's Book.	*tagboard* *handout*
Closing: Play Tic Tac Toe. Tape different amounts of money into the squares. Teams have to say: "You owe me _____."	*play money*
Evaluation: Respond to the evaluation questions orally using the koosh ball.	*koosh ball*

The popular educator should understand the forms of resistance of the working classes.

. . . .

4. Tenant Rights: Making a Complaint

Theme: Immigrant Rights

Language Objectives

- be able to request that something be fixed
- understand tenant rights

Vocabulary

- toilet, sink, shower, ceiling, refrigerator, stove, oven, door, lock, window, AC, heater, gas, cockroaches, bugs, etc.

Code

Skit

Do a skit about a two people complaining about the conditions in their apartment (no heat, bugs, etc.) and the landlord refusing to fix anything. Start a dialog about the skit using the questions for dialog as a guide.

Questions for Dialog

1. Describe

What happens in the skit?
What are the two people talking about?
What is wrong in their apartment?

2. Interpret and Relate

Why do you think there are so many problems in their apartment?
Whose responsibility is it to fix these problems?
Why do you think the landlord won't fix the problems?
Do you know anyone who has had a problem like this?

3. Analyze and Act

What other kinds of problems exist in our apartments?
What can we do to resolve a problem like the one in the skit?
How can we learn more about tenant rights?

Activities	Materials
Warm-Up: Sequencing Activity: Prepare flashcards with words that make simple sentences such as "I live in Maryland." Invite small groups to put the words in order.	*flashcards*
Code: Facilitate a discussion about the skit using the questions for dialog as a guide.	
Speaking & Listening *Activity #1: New Vocabulary* 1. Show or draw pictures of apartment vocabulary. 2. Point to the objects and say the words. 3. Point to pictures of vocabulary and say, "My _____ is broken." *Activity #2: Role Play* 1. Demonstrate a dialog of a tenant talking with a landlord about a problem in his/her apartment. 2. Invite a volunteer to take the place of the tenant. 3. Invite a volunteer to take the place of the landlord.	*pictures* *pictures*
Break	
Reading & Writing *Activity #1: Dialog* 1. Write the apartment dialog on the board. 2. Read the dialog chorally and in pairs. 3. Erase key words from the dialog. 4. Invite volunteers to write the new words. *Activity #2 Sequencing Activity* 1. Ask each participant to copy one of the sentences from the dialog onto tagboard. 2. Participants hold up sentences and read chorally. 3. Shuffle the sentences and invite group to put in order.	*tagboard*
Closing: Guide participants through the worksheet on p.89 of the Student's Book.	*handout*
Evaluation: Play music. Pass ball in a circle. When music stops, person with the ball answers evaluation question.	*tape recorder* *koosh ball*

Notes

Improving Health and Safety

Theme: Health and Safety

Content

AIDS

Getting Sick

Health Clinics

Reading Labels

Alcoholism

Unit Goal

In this unit, we will study the health and safety hazards affecting the Latino community. As a part of our study, we will analyze common myths surrounding diseases such as AIDS and alcoholism. We will also share information about existing community resources.

1. Acting Against AIDS
Theme: Health and Safety

Language Objectives
- ✎ be able to recognize and say the letters of the alphabet
- ✎ be able to identify forms of the verb "to be"

Vocabulary
- ✍ AIDS/HIV, condoms, sex, drugs, needles, etc.

Code

Questions for Dialog

1. Describe
What do we see in the picture?
What is the woman in the picture holding?
How is the man reacting?

2. Interpret and Relate
Why does the woman want to use a condom?
Why does the man react so strongly against using a condom?
What do we know about AIDS? What does the word mean? What is HIV?
Who do you think this disease affects?
How is the disease spread?

3. Analyze and Act
How can we prevent the spread of the HIV virus?
What is our community doing to address this problem?
What can we do as a group to help solve this problem?

Activities	Materials
Warm-Up: Ball toss: What's your name? How do you spell that? Take turns spelling names on the board.	*koosh ball*
Code: Facilitate a discussion about the drawing on p.86 using the questions for dialog as a guide.	*drawing*
Speaking & Listening *Activity #1: The Alphabet* 1. Write the word AIDS on the board. Ask group: "How do you say these letters in English?" 2. Group practices spelling AIDS. 3. What is AIDS in Spanish? What does AIDS stand for? 4. Write out Acquired Immune Deficiency Syndrome on the board. 5. Practice spelling chorally and in pairs. *Activity #2: Idea Web* 1. Ask" "What do you think of when you hear the word AIDS or SIDA?" Group responds in English or Spanish. 2. Make an idea web with AIDS as the trigger word. 3. Write ideas on the board and draw a line to connect them to the trigger word. 4. Practice spelling the new words. 5. Practice the alphabet from A-Z.	
Break	
Reading & Writing *Activity #1: Reading a Story* 1. Read the story from p.97 of the Student's Book out loud. 2. Participants underline words they don't know. 3. Participants spell new words orally while you write them on the board. 4. Help group in defining new vocabulary. *Activity #2: Grammar Work* 1. Ask group if it sees forms of "to be" in the letter. 2. Group circles forms of "to be" in the letter. 3. Read the story chorally and in pairs. *Activity #3: Group Letter* 1. Write a response to the letter as a class. 2. Translate it line by line from Spanish to English. 3. Invite participants to circle forms of "to be" in the letter.	*handout*
Closing: Play hangman or disappearing man with one of the new words.	
Evaluation: Have a discussion about what participants liked and what they didn't like about the class.	

The banking approach will never propose to students that they critically consider reality.

2. Getting Sick

Theme: Health and Safety

Language Objectives

- be able to identify parts of the body
- be able to indicate pain and health problems

Vocabulary

- head, back, throat, ear, arm, leg, etc.
- "What's the matter?" "My _____ hurts."

Code

Skit

Do a skit about a worker getting sick and not going to the doctor because it is too expensive. Start a dialog about the skit using the questions for dialog as a guide.

Questions for Dialog

1. Describe
What happens in the skit?
What is the matter with the person in the skit?
How does the skit end?

2. Interpret and Relate
Why doesn't the person in the skit want to go to the doctor?
Have you ever been sick like this since you've been in this country?
Did you go to the doctor? Why? Why not?

3. Analyze and Act
Why is health care so expensive in this country?
What can we do to reduce our risk of getting sick?
Does anyone know where we can get medical treatment at a low cost?
What else can we do to address this problem?

Activities	Materials
Warm-Up: Error Correction. Write: What your name? Where you from? Where you living? on the board. Participants correct mistakes.	
Code: Facilitate a discussion about the skit using the questions for dialog as a guide.	
Speaking & Listening *Activity #1: TPR* 1. Lead group in a TPR activity with parts of the body. 2. Invite a volunteer to lead the activity. *Activity #2: Koosh Ball* 1. Point to a part of the body and throw the koosh ball to someone. 2. Person who catches the ball says the body part. 3. Continue until group feels comfortable. *Activity #3: TPR* 1. Pantomime a stomach ache. Say: "My stomach hurts." 2. Lead group in TPR using this structure with other body parts. 3. Now introduce "His/Her/Your stomach hurts." 4. Practice with koosh ball.	*koosh ball* *koosh ball*
Break	
Reading & Writing *Activity #1: Group Picture* 1. Draw a picture of yourself on the board. 2. Invite group to help you label the parts of the body. 3. Practice reading the parts of the body. *Activity #2: Matching Game* 1. Participants copy body parts onto index cards. 2. Read through the index cards. 3. Erase the labeled body parts on the picture. 4. Shuffle the cards and participants match the card with the picture. *Activity #3: Cloze* 1. Write the cloze on the board: My _____ hurts. 2. Practice filling in the cloze with the index cards. 3. Now pantomime an ailment and throw the ball to a someone. 4. That person fills in the blank with the index card.	*index cards*
Closing: Have participants pair up. Call out a part of the body. Partners have to connect that body part.	
Evaluation: Write some evaluation questions on the board. Students answer the questions orally using the koosh ball.	*koosh ball*

Liberating education consists of cognition not transferals of information.

3. Going to a Health Clinic
Theme: Health and Safety

Language Objectives

- be able to talk about pain and ailments
- know the vocabulary for parts of the body

Vocabulary

- head, back, ears, stomach, chest, throat, etc.
- "What's the matter?" "I have a stomachache."

Code

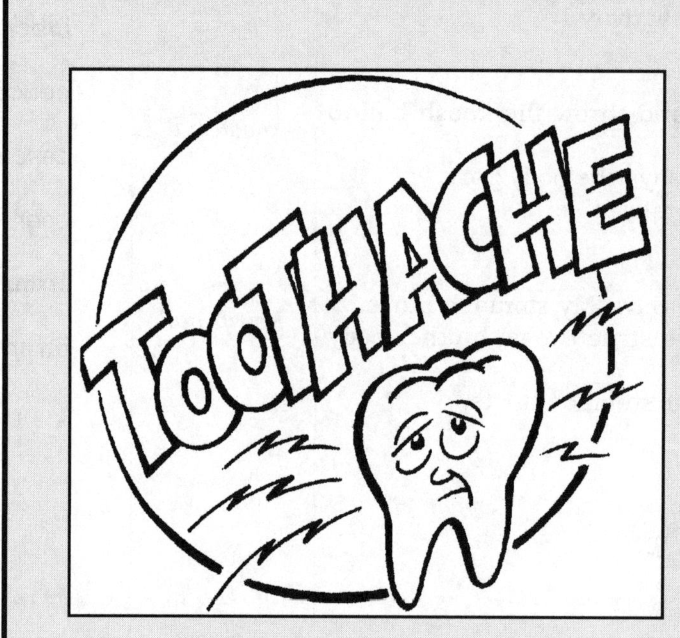

Picture Story

Pass out cut up copies of the picture story, Toothache on p.103 of the Student Book. Students put the story in correct sequence. Start a dialog about the story using the questions for dialog as a guide.

Questions for Dialog

1. Describe

What do we see in the picture story?
What's the matter with the man in the story?
What happens at the end of the story?

2. Interpret and Relate

Why can't the man pay the bill?
Have you ever been sick since you've been in the U.S.?
What did you do?

3. Analyze and Act

What can the man do to solve this problem?
Why is the cost of health care so expensive in this country?
Are their any free health clinics in our neighborhoods?
What can we do as a group to address this problem?

Activities	Materials
Warm-Up: Review parts of the body. Do TPR pointing to body parts. Invite participants to say the commands.	
Code: Facilitate a discussion about the picture story using the questions for dialog as a guide.	*picture story*
Speaking & Listening *Activity #1: TPR* 1. Pantomime a headache and say: "I have a headache." 2. Group imitates action and says: "I have a headache." 3. Repeat with other ailments. 4. Now pantomime an ailment and ask: "What's wrong?" 5. Group responds: "You have a headache." 6. Participants pantomime ailments asking: "What's wrong?" *Activity #2: Role Play* 1. Role play a dialog between a sick person and a nurse at a clinic with the nurse asking: "What's the matter?" 2. Model the dialog with puppets or pictures. 3. Invite participants to take the part of the sick person. 4. Invite participants to take the part of the nurse. 5. Discuss other conversations at a health clinic and role play if you have time.	
Break	
Reading & Writing *Activity #1: Dialog* 1. Ask group to help you write out the dialog from the previous activity. 2. Point to the words and read the dialog chorally and in pairs. 3. Ask each participant to copy one sentence of the dialog onto tagboard. 4. Read the dialog again. 5. Collect the tagboard, shuffle, and invite group to sequence the dialog. *Activity #2: Worksheet* 1. Guide participants through worksheet on p. 102 of the Student's Book.	*tagboard* *handout*
Closing: Do TPR again with parts of the body and ailments.	
Evaluation: Ball Toss: Participants answer the evaluation questions orally.	*koosh ball*

Without democratic intervention there is no progressive education.

4. Reading Prescriptions

Theme: Health and Safety

Language Objectives

✎ be able to read a prescription

Vocabulary

✍ head, back, ears, stomach, chest, throat, etc.

✍ "Take 1 tsp 3 times daily." etc.

Code

Skit

Do a skit about someone getting medicine from the pharmacy, not being able to read the label, and taking too much. Start a dialog about the skit using the questions for dialog as a guide.

Questions for Dialog

1. Describe

What did we see in the skit?
What is the person in the skit doing?
What happens at the end of the skit?

2. Interpret and Relate

What do you think will happen to the person in the skit?
What could the person have done instead?
Have you ever had this problem?

3. Analyze and Act

Do you know any home remedies for the flu or other ailments?
Do you know any over-the-counter medication that you can take?
Who can we ask if we need someone to translate for us?
What else can we do to address this problem?

Activities	Materials
Warm-Up: Review parts of the body. Do TPR with students pointing to body parts. Invite volunteers to lead activity.	
Code: Facilitate a discussion about the skit using the questions for dialog as a guide.	
Speaking & Listening *Activity #1: Game* 1. Point to a teaspoon and say: "This is one teaspoon." 2. Group repeats vocabulary words chorally. 3. Repeat with TBSP, capsules, tablets, etc. 4. Lay the items on the table and say: "Take one _____." 5. Participants grab that item. *Activity #2: Role Play* 1. Role play a dialog between a patient and a doctor with the doctor saying how much medicine the patient should take. 2. Model the dialog with puppets or pictures. 3. Invite volunteer to play the part of the sick person. 4. Invite volunteer to play the part of the doctor. 5. Discuss other conversations at a health clinic and role play if you have time.	*teaspoon* *tablespoon* *tablets* *capsules*
Break	
Reading & Writing *Activity #1: New Vocabulary Cloze* 1. Tape the items on the board. 2. Invite group to help you spell the new words. 3. Point to the vocabulary and say the words. 4. Now write: "Take _____" on the board. 5. Invite the group to take one teaspoon. 6. Volunteers come to the board and fill in the blanks. *Activity #2: Reading a Label* 1. Divide the class into smaller groups. 2. Give each group an empty pill container. 3. Invite groups to try to figure out doses. 4. Ask for help in writing the doses on the board. 5. Make Spanish/English flashcards with the vocabulary. 6. Invite group to draw the flashcards and say what the word is in Spanish.	*pill containers* *index cards*
Closing: Repeat TPR with parts of the body and ailments.	
Evaluation: Ball Toss: Answer the evaluation questions orally.	*koosh ball*

Organizers who hope to educate must increase their historical and cultural sensitivity.

5. Alchohol: How does it affect us?
Theme: Health And Safety

Language Objectives
✎ be able to tell a simple story in English

Vocabulary
✍ story vocabulary

Code

Questions for Dialog

1. Describe
What do we see in the picture?
What is the problem that the picture addresses?

2. Interpret and Relate
Why do you think the men are drinking so much?
What are some signs of alcoholism?
How does alcoholism affect us?
How does it affect our families and our communities?
What role does advertising play in this problem?

3. Analyze and Act
What can we do if we think we have a problem with alcohol?
What can we do if someone we know has a problem?
What can we do as a group to address the problem of alcoholism?

Activities	Materials
Warm-Up: Form a circle and review the days of the week using the koosh ball.	*koosh ball*
Code: Facilitate a discussion about the drawing on p.94 using the questions for dialog as a guide.	*drawing*
Speaking & Listening *Activity #1: LEA Story (part 1)* 1. Ask group if anyone has a story involving the use of drugs or alcohol. 2. Listen to the participant tell the story. 3. Write the story in simple Spanish sentences. 4. Participants draw pictures to illustrate the story. *Activity #2: LEA Story (part 2)* 1. Tape pictures next to the Spanish sentences on the board. 2. Point to pictures and elicit vocabulary. 3. Participants repeat vocabulary. 4. Describe the pictures in simple English sentences. 5. Invite participants to describe the pictures. 6. Invite participants to tell the story in English.	*markers* *paper*
Break	
Reading & Writing *Activity #1: TPR* 1. Tape the pictures of the story on the board. 2. Invite group to help you write a verb for each picture. 3. Read the verbs and point to the pictures. 4. Participants copy the verbs onto index cards. 5. Say a verb and group points to the correct card. 6. Use the verbs to practice telling the story. *Activity #2: Cloze* 1. Ask group to help you write out the story. 2. Read the story chorally and in pairs. 3. Erase the verbs in the story. 4. Invite volunteers to the board to fill in the blanks.	*index cards*
Closing: Koosh Ball: Form a circle and practice the days of the week.	*koosh ball*
Evaluation: Draw a picture of a human figure. How did class affect the participants heads? What about their hearts?	

Notes

Getting Organized

Theme: Solidarity

Content

Day Labor Centers

Organizing an Event

Unit Goal

A strong community is one that is well-organized. In this unit, we will attempt to identify the benefits of group solidarity and compare it with the myth of individualism and the promise of the American Dream.

1. Day Labor Centers
Theme: Solidarity

Language Objectives
- be able to express needs
- "We need _____."

Vocabulary
- trailer, computers, classroom, bathrooms, chairs, etc.

Code

Skit
Do a skit about someone choosing not to use the Day Labor Center because of some problems that exist there. Start a dialog about the skit using the questions for dialog as a guide.

Questions for Dialog

1. Describe
What did we see in the skit?
Why doesn't the worker want to use the day labor center?
What does he choose to do instead?

2. Interpret and Relate
Have you used a day labor center?
What were your experiences?
What are some problems that exist at the center?

3. Analyze and Act
What can we do to address some of the problems at our work centers?
What can we do as a group to make the local, regional and national government aware of the need for organized worker centers?
How can we be better organized as a community of workers?

Activities	Materials
Warm-Up: Do TPR with some common work activities such as painting, breaking concrete, shoveling snow, hammering, etc.	
Code: Facilitate a discussion about the skit using the questions for dialog as a guide.	
Speaking & Listening *Activity #1: Brainstorming* 1. Show group the picture of the day labor center on the cover of this book. Generate "Things at a Center" vocabulary. 2. Ask what you would need to start a new center and draw those things on the board. 3. Point to the pictures and say: "We need a _____." 4. Practice expressing needs with koosh ball. *Activity #2: Rules for a Center* 1. Discuss what rules exist at a center. 2. Translate the rules into English. 3. Say the rules in English and in Spanish. 4. Evaluate each rule. Is this a good idea? Or a bad idea? 5. Group responds: "Yes, it is." "No, it isn't"	*pictures* *koosh ball*
Break	
Reading & Writing *Activity #1: Matching Game* 1. Write the rules onto two sets of index cards, one in English and one in Spanish. 2. Practice reading the rules. 3. Play matching game with the rules. *Activity #2: Worksheet* 1. Now compare the rules with those of other day labor centers. 2. What are the similarities and differences? 3. Guide participants through the worksheet on p. 106 of the Student's Book.	*index cards* *rules handout*
Closing: Take turns saying what you need at a center.	*koosh ball*
Evaluation: Draw some faces on the board: happy, sad, etc. Participants draw faces representing how they felt in class.	

Problem-posing education involves a constant unveiling of realities.

2. Organizing an Event

Theme: Solidarity

Language Objectives

- be able to express needs
- be able to express future tense using "will"

Vocabulary

- common food, music, tape recorder, plates, silverware, etc.

Code

Questions for Dialog

1. Describe
What do we see in the picture?
Who are the people in the picture?
What are the people in the picture doing?

2. Interpret and Relate
How important is it to work together as a group?
What are the benefits of group solidarity?
Can we accomplish more working alone or as a group?
Do you think our community is well-organized?
If so, how did we get organized? If not, why not?

3. Analyze and Act
What are some obstacles preventing us from being united as a community?
How can we overcome these obstacles?
What else can we do to organize our community?

Activities	Materials
Warm-Up: Practice the days of the week. What day is today? What day is tomorrow? What day was yesterday?	*koosh ball*
Code: Facilitate a discussion about the photograph on p.100 using the questions for dialog as a guide.	*photograph*
Reading & Writing *Activity #1: Idea Web* 1. Write the name of the event you want to organize on the board. 2. Ask students: "What do we need for this event?" 3. Connect suggestions with the name of the event in an idea web. 4. Practice saying the new vocabulary. 5. Add: "We need + the new vocabulary." *Activity #2: Koosh Ball* 1. Ask if group knows how to express something in the future in English. 2. Point to something you want to bring and say: "I will bring the _____." 3. Group repeats orally. 4. Now ask what participants want to bring. 5. Volunteers respond: "I will bring the _____."	
Break	
Speaking & Listening *Activity #1: Slapjack* 1. Copy what you are going to bring onto index cards. 2. Hold up cards and take turns saying what you are going to bring. 3. Collect the cards and put them face up on the table. 4. Call out vocabulary and participants grab that card. *Activity #2: Worksheet* 1. Guide participants through the worksheet on p. 108 of the Student's Book. *Activity #3: Writing Project* 1. Write a bilingual invitation to someone the group wants to invite to the event. OR 2. Design a bilingual flyer for the event.	*index cards* *handout*
Closing: Koosh ball: Pass the koosh ball saying what you are going to bring to the event.	*koosh ball*
Evaluation: Ask: "What did you like best about today's class?" And: "What didn't you like?"	

Notes

Making a Better Future

Theme: Social Change

Content

Permanent Jobs

Job Applications

Job Interviews

Goal Setting

Unit Goal

In this unit, we will identify collective goals for the future and look at how our goals are connected with social change. We will analyze obstacles that impede us from achieving our goals and brainstorm ways to overcome these obstacles.

1. Finding a Permanent Job
Theme: Social Change

Language Objectives
- ✎ be able to make a request: "Can I have...?"
- ✎ be able to read help wanted signs

Vocabulary
- ✍ Help Wanted, Prep Cook Needed, Apply Within, etc.

Code

Questions for Dialog

1. Describe
What do we see in the picture?
What are the people in the picture saying?
What's the weather like outside?

2. Interpret and Relate
Why isn't there any work?
What are some other obstacles we face to finding steady work?
Have you ever been in this situation?

3. Analyze and Act
What can the workers in the picture do?
What can we do to change the laws that make it difficult for workers like these to get permanent jobs?
What else can we do as a group to help people in this situation?

Activities	Materials
Warm-Up: Ball Toss: Review clarification language with students. "I don't understand." "Can you repeat that?" etc.	*koosh ball*
Code: Facilitate a discussion about the drawing on p.104 using the questions for dialog as guide.	*drawing*
Speaking & Listening *Activity #1: Matching Exercise* 1. Tape pictures of day labor jobs in columns on the board. 2. Hold up prepared Help Wanted signs matching the pictures. 3. Go over the vocabulary on the signs with the group. 4. Ask group: "What kind of work is it?" 5. Match the sign with the picture. *Activity #2: Role Play* 1. Role play a dialog between someone looking for a job and an employer. 2. Focus first on requesting an application. 3. Model the dialog with pictures or puppets. 4. Invite a volunteer to take the place of the worker. 5. Invite a volunteer to take the place of the employer 6. Practice the dialog in pairs.	*pictures* *signs*
Break	
Reading & Writing *Activity #1: Dialog Cloze* 1. Write out the dialog from the previous activity. 2. Read the dialog as a group and in pairs. 3. Now erase key words in the dialog. 4. Volunteers come to the board and fill in the blanks. *Activity #2: Worksheet* 1. Guide participants in completing the worksheet on p. 118 of the Student's Book.	 *handout*
Closing: Play hangman or disappearing man using the new vocabulary.	
Evaluation: Ball Toss: Participants say one thing that they learned in class.	*koosh ball*

Without love,
the process of
popular education
would lose
its meaning.

2. Filling out Job Applications

Theme: Social Change

Language Objectives

✎ be able to give and request personal information

✎ be able to fill out a simple information form

Vocabulary

✍ first name, last name, address, city, state, zip code, salary, etc.

Code

Skit

Do a skit about someone wanting to apply for a job but being intimidated by the application. Start a dialog about the skit using the questions for dialog as a guide.

Questions for Dialog

1. Describe

What happens in the skit?
What is the person doing? What's the problem?
What happens at the end of the skit?

2. Interpret and Relate

Why is the person in the skit applying for the job?
Why doesn't he/she fill out the application?
What can he/she do to overcome this obstacle?
What can you do if you have this problem?

3. Analyze and Act

What are some other obstacles we face in trying to get a permanent job?
Why do these obstacles exist?
What can we do as a community to overcome these obstacles?

Activities	Materials
Warm-Up: Write simple questions such as, "What is your name?" and "Where do you live?" Cut up the sentences into single word flashcards. Group sequences the flashcards.	*flashcards*
Code: Facilitator leads a discussion about the skit using the questions for dialog as a guide.	
Speaking & Listening *Activity #1: Ball Toss* 1. Review giving personal information. 2. Begin by modeling: "My first name is _____." 3. Group practices with koosh ball. 4. When group feels comfortable, add: "My last name is _____." 5. Repeat with phone number, address, etc. *Activity #2: Chain Drill* 1. Form a circle. 2. Facilitator models possessive adjectives: (My name/His name/Her name) 3. Do a chain drill with personal information. ("My name is _____ and her name is _____.")	*koosh ball*
Break	
Reading & Writing *Activity #1: Matching Game* 1. Ask group to think of things on a job application. (First Name, Last Name, Address, Salary, etc.) 2. Group helps you translate into English. 3. Brainstorm corresponding information (i.e. $10/hr for salary) and write examples on the board. 4. Participants copy information onto two sets of index cards. 5. Play matching game. *Activity #2: Worksheet* 1. Copy the job application from p. 115 in the Student's Book on the board. 2. Group helps you fill out the application. 3. Guide participants in filling out the job application on p.100 of the Student's Book	*index cards* *handout*
Closing: Ball toss: Participants say one thing that is on a job application.	*koosh ball*
Evaluation: Group forms two concentric circles. Participants face each other and discuss evaluation question. Circles rotate.	

A humanizing education is the path through which men and women become conscious about their presence in the world.

3. Job Interview
Theme: Social Change

Language Objectives
✎ be able to ask and respond to questions in a job interview

Vocabulary
✍ "Do you have any experience?" "When can you start?" "Can you _____?" "How much do you pay?" "Are there breaks?" "Do I get benefits?"

Code

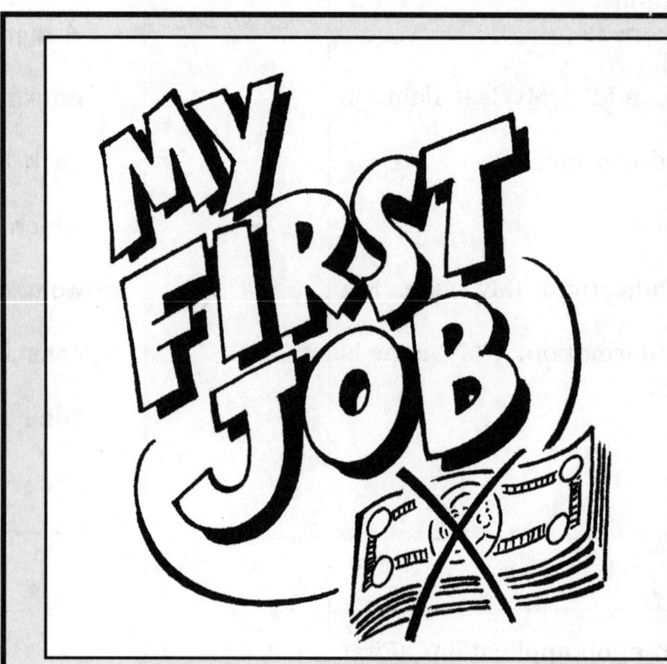

Picture Story

Pass out the picture story *My First Job* on p. 39 of the Student's Book to small groups. Start a dialog about the story using the questions for dialog as a guide.

Questions for Dialog

1. Describe
What happens in the story?
What is the man in the story doing? What is the problem?
What happens at the end of the story?

2. Interpret and Relate
Why doesn't the man get paid for the work that he does?
What can he do to overcome this obstacle?
What can you do if you have this problem?

3. Analyze and Act
Why doesn't the person in the story have a green card?
Why is this problem so widespread in our community?
What can we do to help people with this problem?
What can we do to fight for amnesty and residency for undocumented workers?

Activities	Materials
Warm-Up: Chain drill: Practice expressing needs: "I need _____ and he needs _____."	*koosh ball*
Code: Facilitate a discussion about the picture story using the questions for dialog page as a guide.	*picture story*
Speaking & Listening *Activity #1: Brainstorm* 1. Brainstorm questions employers ask in a job interview. 2. Group helps translate three or four of the questions into English. 3. Practice saying the questions together in English 4. Brainstorm possible answers to the questions. 5. Practice asking and answering the questions with the koosh ball. 6. Practice asking and answering in pairs. *Activity #2: Role Play* 1. Group role plays a job interview. 2. Begin by modeling the interview with pictures or puppets. 3. Invite a volunteer to play the role of the person looking for a job. 4. Volunteers play both roles.	*koosh ball*
Break	
Reading & Writing *Activity #1: Sentence Scramble* 1. Group copies each word of one of the questions onto separate index cards. 2. Shuffle the cards and ask group to try to unscramble the question. 3. Repeat with other questions. *Activity #2: Mock Interview* 1. Participants copy all interview questions onto an index card. 2. Higher level and lower level participants pair up for interview. 3. Pairs note down answers on their cards. 4. When pairs finish interviews, they can report back to the group.	*index cards* *index cards*
Closing: Ball toss: Say one question that is asked in an interview.	*koosh ball*
Evaluation: Form two concentric circles. Face each other and discuss evaluation question. Circles rotate to discuss new question.	

Education is a political act.

4. Our Goals for the Future

Theme: Social Change

Language Objectives

✎ be able to talk about our goals for the future
✎ be able to use the future form of "will"

Vocabulary

✍ get a better job; improve my English; become a better carpenter, etc.

Code

Questions for Dialog

1. Describe

What do we see in the picture?
What are some of the obstacles in the road?
What is at the end of the road?

2. Interpret and Relate

What is a goal?
What are some of our goals for the future?
Are our goals for the most part collective or individual goals?
What are some obstacles that we face in achieving our goals?

3. Analyze and Act

How can we work to overcome these obstacles?
What is the best way of working to achieve our goals?
What can we do as a group and as a community to achieve our goals?

Activities	Materials
Warm-Up: Do TPR with common work verbs such as paint, dig, cut, hammer, rake, sweep, etc.	
Code: Facilitate a discussion about the drawing on p.110 using the questions for dialog as a guide.	*drawing*
Speaking & Listening *Activity #1: Brainstorm* 1. Under the heading "The Future", divide the board into three sections: 6 months/1 year/5 years. 2. Say a six-month goal: "In six months I will/want to _____." 3. Draw a picture of your goal in the six-month section. 4. Invite participants to say their six-month goals. 5. Draw pictures of goals and practice: "I will/I want to _____." 6. Repeat with one-year and five-year goals. *Activity #2: Pictures* 1. Draw pictures of goals onto index cards. 2. Hold up the pictures and say your goals: "I want to _____." 3. Collect the cards, shuffle and make a pile. 4. Participants draw from the pile and say the goal on the card. 5. Review 3rd person singular when talking about someone else's goals.	*index cards*
Break	
Reading & Writing *Activity #1: Writing Activity* 1. Write out one of the goals into the columns on the board. 2. Point to the goal and read it chorally. 3. Discuss what you need to be able to achieve your goals. What are some obstacles you face? Who can help you? 4. Copy goals onto tagboard. 5. Read the tagboard together and as a group. *Activity #2: Worksheet* 1. Guide participants through worksheet on p. 121 of the Student's Book.	*tagboard* *handout*
Closing: Play Tic Tac Toe: Tape the pictures in the squares. Teams make sentences to express goals.	
Evaluation: Pass the koosh ball and respond to the evaluation questions.	*koosh ball*

Notes

Unit Reflection

Write your ideas, impressions, and reflections about this unit. If you need more space, keep a reflection journal. Use the questions to help you get started....

The Theme
Write your ideas about the theme in this unit.

Do you identify with the theme? Why? Why not?

What did you learn from the other participants in the group about the theme?

The Codes
What were your impressions about the codes in this unit and the questions about the codes?

Did the codes promote an open dialog about the theme?

What other codes could you have used to reach an analysis of the same theme?

Unit Reflection

Activities

Which activities in this unit did the group respond best to? Which were least successful? Why?

What other activities could you have used to achieve the same language objectives?

Participation

Did all members of the group participate in activities in this unit? Did the men and the women participate equally?

What can you do to increase and balance the level of participation of all members of the group?

Learning

When did the most significant learning take place in this unit?

What can you change or improve to increase the impact of learning on the group in the next unit?

What can you do to learn more about popular education and bring back what you've learned to the group?

Bibliography

Auerbach, Elsa, Making Meaning, Making Change, Center for Applied Linguistics and Delta Systems, McHenry, IL, 1992.

Freire, Paulo, Education for Critical Consciousness, Continuum, New York, NY, 1973.

Freire, Paulo, Pedagogy of the Oppressed, Continuum, New York, NY, 1970.

Freire, Paulo, Teachers as Cultural Workers, Westview Press, Boulder, Colorado, 1998.

Gómez, Gloria, et. al. Vamos a Jugar: Juegos y Dinámicas para la Educación, No. 1., Asociación Equipo Maíz, San Salvador, El Salvador, 1999.

Gómez, Gloria, et. al. Vamos a Jugar Otra Vez: Juegos y Dinámicas para la Educación, No. 2., Asociación Equipo Maíz, San Salvador, El Salvador, 2000.

IDEPSCA, Guía para la Cartilla de Alfabetización de IDEPSCA, Instituto de Educación Popular del Sur de California, Los Angeles, CA.

Ligon, Fred, et. al. More Picture Stories: Language and Problem-Posing Activities for Beginners, Longman Publishing Group, White Plains New York, 1992.

Romero, Elmer, et. al., Harina para mi costal: una exeriencia de educación popular en El Salvador, Asociación Equipo Maíz, San Salvador, El Salvador, 2000.

Stern, Hilary, et. al. A Curriculum for Migrant Latino Workers, CASA Latina, Seattle, WA, 1996.